james

THE MAN BOOK

**If
you're
interested
in
being
a
man . . .**

The Man Book

Copyright © 2010, 2015 by Makin' A Hand Publishing. All Rights Reserved.

For information about this title or to order other books and/or electronic media, contact the publisher:
Makin' A Hand Publishing
prairie1943@gmail.com

ISBN: 978-0-9861583-0-8

Printed in the United States of America
Cover and Interior design: 1106 Design

In Praise Of All Women, Love's Teachers

In Praise Of All Men:
They Learned To Love
Deeply

With Hope
For All Young Males
&
All Young Females
&
All Aging Males and Females
Interested In Becoming Men and Women

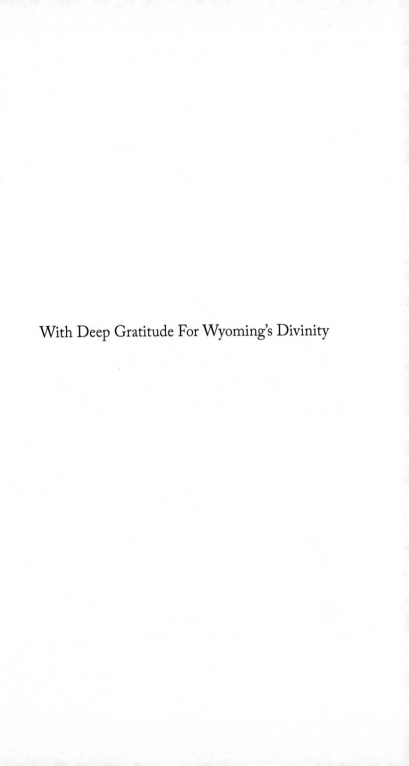

With Deep Gratitude For Wyoming's Divinity

Of love and desire let no man speak
Until their union has made him weak.

QUALIFICATIONS FOR WRITING THIS BOOK:

- Birth
- Abuse
- Survival
- A Father In Deep Destruction
- A Mother In Deep Dishonor
- Beatings
- Russian Roulette
- Family Alcoholism
- Poverty
- Homelessness
- Will To Survive
- Hard Work
- Love For Living & Laughter
- Isolation

- Confusion
- Studying
- Determination To Survive
- Hard Work
- No Drugs
- No Alcohol
- No Excuses
- No Shortcuts
- No Anesthesia
- No Mentors
- Studying & Teaching
- Bad Boy: Shame, Guilt, Regrets
- Survival As Deep As It Goes
- Curiosity
- Searching
- Hitchhiking
- Jail
- Marriage
- Fatherhood
- Divorce
- Hard Work & Self-discipline & Personal Vows
- Studying & Teaching Humbly

- Dreams & Education All Life Long
- Gratitude To Every Writer, Artist, Composer, & Musician Who Influenced Me
- Gratitude For Every Person Who Tried To Love Me
- Gratitude For Every Person Who Succeeded
- Gratitude For Every Person Who Resisted
- Laughter & Play All Life Long But With Difficulties
- Two Adored Daughters, Two Adored Grandchildren
- Studying & Teaching Even More Humbly
- Wyoming All Life Long
- Luck As Blessings
- Adventures & Risks
- Deaths
- Play
- Making Dreams Come True
- Cancer
- Trying To Marry Reality & Remarry It More Deeply
- God Naked Unto Faith
- Professor Emeritus

- The Giving Of Thanks Through Giving
- Learning To Lead With Love So Love Can Follow
- Learning To Follow Love So Love Can Lead
- Mistakes
- Defeats
- Failures
- Stirrups
- Bareback
- Pain
- Beauty
- Seeking
- Trying to Learn How to Weigh Wind....

&

Riding Bulls

CONTENTS

EVERY CHILD is holiness.

The destiny of every child is to pass through gender to stature: from male/female to man/woman. The passage is challenging. Few seek it. Few complete it.

This book focuses on the male journey into the realities of becoming a man.

Therefore, the contents are:

An Introductory Overview

I'm older.
In my slang that means a lotta rodeos.

With that in mind, what do I really know after all these years?

Well, I know the obvious facts and a lot of information.

But what interests me most is *'connecting the dots'*: the paradoxes and beauties of living, the confusions of thinking and loving, and the inevitable hardships of maturing that put all of us and our dreams on ice and flame, ocean and desert—in all conditions of reality and spirit where freedom, liberty, and finitude make us reflect with perplexity and hope, fear and anxiety, bravery and courage, ignorance and certainty, tears and joy.

I also know:

- ✦ the central dot of this book is the destiny of the male.

- ✦ the fullest destiny for all males is to become a man.

- ✦ being a man transcends image, job, wealth, sexual orientation, religion, race, influence, possessions, and winning.

But what do I *really* know?

Well, right now I know I'm going to write this book.

So here goes....

I know words never quite define truth to Truth. And I also know that words used positively and honestly represent the best attempts to complete aspects of that beautifully difficult effort. Enhancing the ability to 'see' the truly true and learning to place words in sequences that duplicate the truly true structures of visible and invisible reality so meanings can be perceived, interpreted, reinterpreted, appreciated, and lived—I know that's the most creative use of language.

i believe....

- ✦ Life seeks us. And, as you know, we respond to life by trying to actualize our potential through living. We are free to do that and not to do that.

+ Free means we think, imagine, wonder, and *choose*. Choosing is problematic until we learn how to 'see' more realistically and think better. This represents growth toward maturity. The ideal result of maturity is consistency of truly responsible decisions resulting in the good.

+ Choosing is partially governed by the scope of one's liberty—the options defined by all aspects of living that influence thinking and feeling.

+ Choosing is derived from reasoning as forethought, little thought, too much thought, or no deliberation at all—impulse.

+ Choosing is based on reducing options to immediate alternatives that boil down to a simple 'yes' or 'no'. Each answer sets different realities in motion toward the truly positive, some form of mistake, or into something bad—the negative. That's the risk of choosing.

+ Risk is impossible to avoid.

+ The avoidance of risk is even riskier. To avoid basic risk causes a drift into personal staleness and degrees of resignation and resistance that usually lead to some form of doubt, indifference, personal stagnation, deeper resignation, and, eventually, spiritual decline. Without taking risks, you will become deeply bored and equally boring—no 'growth'.

No growth, no love.
No love, no vitality.
No vitality, you check out early and wait to die.

✦ No other creature is so *free,* so free to think and *seek,* and so free to *speak* instead of utter.

We can touch W.B. Yeats' 'cloths of heaven'.
We can destroy those cloths, and we do.

This book is partially about touching that heavenly cloth, then learning how to hold on to it for keeps.

✦ The truth and beauty of language is easily and wonderfully observable when a child, after months of sound patterning, coordinates with the real, begins to 'get it', and utters first words *knowingly.* Then the journey into reasoning begins. It moves the child from pure curiosity—the sublime unity of ignorance and potential—toward actualizing the beauty of awareness called *learning through play.* The miracle-mix of curiosity, play, and language slowly *takes* the child *into personal creativity,* the state of being lured by the possible *all the time.*

✦ The dynamism of *play* is creativeness that will, if appropriately guided and sustained, become a major influence on the process of maturing. In this sense, increasingly mature play is the core of the spiritual, superficially and profoundly, positively and negatively.

I know play is a key emphasis in this book.
So is learning.

What else do I *really* know?
Well, I know the word 'meaning' is one word no human can dismiss.

I know the purpose of living is to put the truly positive front and center so some light can be made, some true love shared. That effort represents the most sophisticated actions of play.

I know the use of invented facts makes us partially blind to realities and greater meanings. And I know:

Greater persons are aligned with greater meanings.
Lesser persons are aligned with lesser meanings.

I know I can't please every reader. And I know wind is blowing harder and bringing thunder and rain within the hour.

to reiterate:

+ The core of freedom is awareness and decisions.

+ Freedom basically is a state of tension related to altering reality for the possible.

+ Confused thinking or thinking guided by too much thinking, feeling, and/or ignorance causes the tail to wag the dog. Dog loses.

+ Learning *how to think* and *how to love* better are the only ways to reduce losses caused by mismanaged thinking and loving.

+ Being a man is a serious topic.

that said....

This book is a positive effort. It's not a lecture, an attempt to please you, mentor you, or entertain you. Think of it as a friendly intrusion centered on the wish to encourage rather than offend and contribute rather than alienate, criticize, or condemn.

So....

Writing this book feels like wrapping a gift. I hope all the fragments and their numerous reiterations will encourage you to do the unwrap and explore what it really means to be a complete man.

more specifically....

This book is for males who never gave much thought to the question of manhood, for males who falsely claim to be men, for males who would like to be men, for aging males who need to be more interested in complete manhood, and for all younger males who have no idea what a man is and can't find a resource for clarification, simplicity, and guidance.

So, if you're a younger male or an aging male over thirty and you're determined to and able to dismiss the relevancy of the question and criteria of manhood, put this book down. You're not ready. Let it be. Accept that your mind is partially numb to the facts and truths this book explores. You'll want to argue, dismiss what bothers you, defend yourself, and criticize me or the writing. The point is, you won't be *willing* to see beyond your fears, biases, preferences, assumptions, ignorance, negative stubbornness, influences, habits, conclusions, passivity, and insecurities regarding matters of honesty, manhood, and personal growth. You'll protect yourself in ways that will spare you from acknowledging your confusion, shallowness, and the pain of learning that your mindset is partially ignorant, self-deceptive, and in service to active or passive denial, avoidance, arrogance, and habits.

I call this kind of aloofness and arrogance 'finessed cowardice'.

There are many ways to finesse cowardly aloofness. This book addresses those disguises.

however....

If you *are* willing to roll with the question of manhood, keep reading.

Then go to a mirror and have a little talk about what you think strength and courage are. And cowardice. And love.

Then talk bluntly and openly about your own courage, cowardliness, strength, and love.

Take notes. Try to define the words.

Then take the notes and definitions to a friend, mate, partner, or wife.

Read them aloud and converse honestly.

Then think aloud about your manhood and maturity.

+ If you dismiss all that activity and return to your trance, good luck. You'll need luck because all trances are forms of self-incarceration through lies. Lies cause self-waste and interpersonal losses due to *fear of real reality and the new*: change.

+ If you're a finessed coward, please know you've developed simple, clever, and/or defensive rationales that preclude deeper self-honesty related to the truly valid personal growth this book explores.

✦ If you're willing to acknowledge any kind of personal trance, you're in position to initiate valid adventures for discovering more about what being a man entails.

that said....

We all know there's a surplus of males, a scarcity of men. It's a global fact.

And we know that global misery is due to male mismanagement of self, others, ideas, natural resources, facts, money, and truths.

But aging males usually don't want to discuss their cowardice or confront it. Why? Deep honesty isn't on the agenda, that's why.

All of this relates to the eventual and inevitable self-assessment that comes with aging. Sooner or later, you'll think about how you're living and how you've lived. One day you'll ask, what am I really doing, what am I making, have I made anything so far that's really worthwhile, and what would I like to say I've done before I die?

This book is partly asking you those questions.

SO....

If in any way you've become apathetically active, arrogant, complacent, lazy, aimless, lost, cynical, stingy, cheap, smugly tolerant, depressed, discouraged, or intolerantly critical with or without much humor—if any of that's happened in your world, you're missing out on what is yours to learn and do. Unintentionally, maybe you've developed cowardice and you use weak reasoning forcefully or defensively, passively or cleverly, or sarcastically to resist acknowledging your cowardice.

Or you never really questioned yourself deeply enough or long enough to discover any need for real, lasting, valid alterations of self for self-renewal—growth.

Or no one gave you a reality check.

Or you couldn't-wouldn't-didn't-won't listen.

Or maybe you're fairly content now and this book seems extraneous. That's okay. Pass on it. Put the book down.

But if you're curious and not passive, it's time to....

Go A Little Deeper

some facts:

✦ Self-lies initiate self-waste.
How much self-waste you make is your choice.

✦ Deep self-honesty initiates healing.
How much love and goodness you make is your choice.

✦ It's never too late until it's too late.

✦ Most persons unintentionally make less of living because they didn't learn how to think and love more fully, had little training for reality, didn't seek integrity deeply enough, weren't really careful for justice, and settled for too little or reached for too much, didn't reach at all, or, tragically, couldn't.

✦ Your thinking is based on what has influenced you, starting with your parents or whoever was responsible for you when you were little; then what influenced you and how did you respond? Check all that out. See what you come up with.

✦ If you really want to survive the disappointments and difficulties of living, keep a genuine sense of humor, stay resilient, be patient, highly realistic, and decisive; work hard for your dreams, and make demands on yourself to change for the better—away from the stupid, the negative, and the scariness of making sacrifices for the greater good.

This introduces the word *volition*.

✦ Most folks don't respond positively to the demand for self-renewal, the hard work of deep personal change. It's easier to do the familiar, criticize, or buy something than it is to change how you function.

✦ Most folks just get up in the morning, urinate, defecate, eat something, begin routines, work energetically or not or partially, relate to others mechanically, comparatively, courteously, enviously, willingly, or desirously, eat some lunch, complete errands, seek entertainment, have some dinner, and sleep again with or without love in the same dwelling and bed.

this means....

Variations on a theme of 'rut' too often go unquestioned and unchallenged.

Rut is a signal of personal blindness related to preventable but predictable tragedy as losses of self, time, and love. If you've got rut, get help for it. Or stay in your habits until old-age rut demands its full price and you can't pay up or ask for a discount. Rut got too deep.

more ifs....

If you're a male in the trance of claiming to be a man simply because you're past thirty, this book will challenge you.

If you respond positively to the challenge, you'll know this book's intent.

If you respond negatively, you'll remain busily or passively self-wasteful, defensively dishonest, and resistant to maturing. The end result will be more regret, confusion, denial, anger, frustration, suffering, resignation, and a reduced capacity to enjoy living.

Guaranteed: you'll become just another aging male making peace with what you did....but still not doing what you need to do.

If you're a male in the trance of using attitude, your job, possessions, recognition, money, appearance, swearing, humor, reputation, or fighting to secure your sense of power, you're a pretend man: you don't have any real power except potentially. You're in hiding, believing others can't see the pose. If you can't admit that, you won't be able to roll with what I'm writing. You won't be able to admit you walk on stilts.

Guaranteed: all stilt-walkers fall, and the taller the stilts, the longer and harder the fall. There's a real link connecting the word *hubris* to debris.

But if you're a young male who *is* willing and ready to explore how to become a man, then read openly and discover how ready *you-really-are* to embrace the disciplines of mind, body, and spirit related to the truly true and the actions the truly true demands.

a few man facts:

No man calls himself a man. He calls himself by his given name.

No man brags or is falsely impressed.

No man longs to be other than he is.

No man seeks approval.

No man is offended.

No man envies.

No man panics.

No man is vain—fearful of exclusion or rejection.

No man is a fool for love or afraid of deep love.

a few male facts:

Males usually choose paths of conformist success comprised of minor accomplishments celebrated as achievements.

Males not fully interested in becoming complete men do not experience *deep achievement* or much self-fulfillment.

Males avoid full self-confrontation related to failure, defeat, and the mistakes caused by *inappropriate immaturity*. Once informed about what to do, the male who's interested in maturing will find a way to take action for self-alteration or he'll pass on the opportunity.

Males seek endorsement of manliness or, sadly, they shrug it off because they think there's no self-manliness to endorse.

Males who feel deficient often try to develop some kind of 'personal power' in ways that are controllable for self-control and the control of others directly, indirectly, or manipulatively.

Males can't distinguish much real difference between force and power.

Males don't understand that they're basically powerless even though they may be forceful, energetic, adamant, really busy, influential, financially successful, and determined to stay that way.

Males are usually more helpless and vulnerable to criticism than they know or admit, so they do tough or aloof or humor or aggressive or win or sarcasm or some brand of imitative cool to prevent intimacies that would cause them to feel vulnerable and needy, weaker, and more lost than found.

Men know how to deal with forceful males.

consider:

Be-ing a man—the 'do-ing' of it—is 100 percent *until you die*. If you back off at any point, you didn't make the journey. You have to hang in and learn, learn, learn. It's that simple, that hard, and that *good*. No games, no excuses, and no reduction of striving during the lifelong process of seeking 'personal mastery' out of which comes the final domain of 'free' and its spiritual challenges.

One of those challenges is realistic wisdom—the unifications of 'heaven and earth' actively preserved through actions of goodness related to local facts, ultimate truths, and children.

You pass wisdom and goodness on in the best ways you can.

Somehow, you teach.

Encouragement....

If you're a father in any way, read carefully and answer honestly.

If you're a leader in any way, read carefully and answer honestly.

If you're interested in becoming a man, read slowly and be honest.

Otherwise, go have that private conversation in the mirror. Talk out loud. If you have the guts and willingness to do that, then *admit* your cowardice, *reassess* how you abuse yourself and others, and *admit* that you lie. And while you're talking to yourself, nod in agreement that there's no real escape from the fact that you are, one way or another, negatively selfish.

Finally, *conclude* that you're weak in particular ways and unwilling to embrace the facts that deep self-honesty is inseparable from integrity, that integrity serves dignity, and that honesty, integrity, and dignity depend on action.

If you can't go to the mirror and begin to say it like it is, then tell yourself you don't really care about all this, that what I'm writing is irrelevant. Walk away, go watch television, have a glass of wine. Text someone. Restart your trance and chill out.

The relatedness of integrity and dignity is the basic moral code of a man because a man approaches self, others, and the planet with *respect*, the *desire* to see all the lies, and the will to do the *good*.

What is integrity? What is dignity?

Man facts:

A man is willing to learn.

A man studies facts to learn truths.

A man studies until he dies.

A man dies sustaining his commitment to integrity and dignity.

A man is willing to change to conform to the demands for a greater presence of realistic love in all relationships.

Consider....

Love. What is it? And what is self-love?

Folks use the word and phrase a lot.

Try to define and explain love and self-love without stammering.

For starters, self-love presupposes the reality of love and the reality of self.

Self is the result of transcending your identity: becoming truly you, a whole self in stable readiness for other-love: relationship.

If you can't-don't-won't really clarify what love is and isn't, you won't become a cohesive self and you won't love anyone deeply. You'll just feel that way once in awhile, in and out, off and on. Eventually, you'll probably live alone, with or without another person, and get a pet.

Self-love requires *truly valid* self-respect and self-value.

What is love? Is love your first priority?

If it's not your first priority by the time you hit forty, figure out what that means and you'll be able to predict aspects of your future.

As you know by now, I believe....

✦ Learning *how to think* more accurately in order *to make better decisions* is the major challenge of living and loving.

✦ Any passivity regarding learning how to think and love more accurately and deeply represents the core of complacent ignorance and preventable loss.

So consider....

Valid communication of love requires genuine and consistent *proof of love*. This makes the continuity of trust possible.

Trust is love's heartbeat: surrender without submission.

No action is more powerful than personal surrender to goodness.

Goodness points directly and clearly to love and what love is.

Goodness done is love *made*.

Goodness is love's mail. Our job is to make it genuinely and deliver it daily.

We were born for goodness. We were born to love. We were born to deliver.

To lose goodness or love is to lose the opportunity to deliver.

Definition:

Love is radically misunderstood, misinterpreted, misdirected, and misapplied. Yet everyone who is sane agrees that love ultimately is the major beauty of being alive. But what is it? What *is* love?

Most abstractly, it's the ultimate reality in the question of God.

Most concretely, it's the only answer to the question of God.

Most simply, it is ubiquitously present in all meanings.

Most meaningfully, it is Creation within each of us. We are it—love's synonym, mirror, analogue. So we have to do it, do realistic love or accept shrinkage.

If you believe otherwise, you're messed up.

Facts:

Maturity isn't automatic. It must be sought.

Maturing signifies the ongoing perception and integration of greater meanings in all relationships.

Greater meanings activate our inherent greatness because they're in us already.

Greater meanings embody power. Their power as potential for life resides in us, waiting for arousal and placement in living. That's what deep education is all about—making meanings concrete, *lived*. That means shared.

Enhanced 'greatness' depends on thinking and doing what the *will to mature* requires—dealing with reality, self, and others honestly, thoroughly, strongly, creatively, and with accurate aim.

In this sense, moral, mature, and love are active synonyms.

Men know this and live it.

Men are deeply and powerfully volitional.

Males are, in varying degrees, forcefully volitional. Or passive.

A side note....

Most words are spoken with vague specificity and assumed clarity. This leads to the trap of lazy thinking, emotionalized logic, erroneous conclusions, and un-discussed assumptions manifest as assertions, criticisms, opinions, closed questions, closed answers, and rigid solutions. Tail wags the dog. Dog loses. So do the pups.

What's missing in all this? Humility is missing.
And so is substance over content.
Content and substance are not the same.
Like bright and smart are not the same.
What is humility?

Related to tail wagging the dog, consider:

+ Defensiveness is negative assertiveness. What's negated? The *truly* positive is negated: the possibility to *pro-gress* is lost.

+ Assess the presence of self-honesty in persons you know and say you love.

+ There are many kinds of liars and lies. Lying is part of a global sickness.

+ When perceptions of reality become distorted, assumptions aren't discussed, opinions and facts are defended as truths, and genuine questions aren't addressed openly. When any of this goes on, it's negative stubbornness—resistance that blocks the possibilities for better results.

+ Negatively stubborn folks tend to deny their negative stubbornness. They think their 'attitude' and behavior are ok and unrelated to anxiety, fear, and weakness. It's real hard for the negatively stubborn to 'see' what I'm writing about because one result of negative stubbornness is spiritual blindness—the absence of deep self-honesty.

+ Arrested or irregular development in learning how to think and love guarantees you will become stunted. Stunted causes major loss of potential. Loss of potential guarantees unhappiness: more sorrow, only itty-bitty joy, and less self-fulfillment. The living evidence of all this is the aging male and aging female.

All men and women marry life before marrying a mate. That's a big step. Without that action, there's only wedlock.

Males and females do wedlock and call it marriage. Sooner or later, they usually wish to undo the lock. So they hang in, make do, lie, try to work it out, marry life and grow into their wedding vows, or get a divorce.

Men and women wed without the lock.

Reiteration of facts:

If you're truly not interested in becoming a man, you'll accept maleness and the permanent reality of your cowardice: you'll mask fear and helplessness with excessive assertiveness, disregard, or resignation, and you'll do some costume and imitative behavior; you'll do some false humility often and extra courtesies you don't mean, and you'll express sentimental or false love instead of valid, deep love. Eventually, you'll learn how you traded greater love for soft or hard lies and kept your thinking stable with resistance and rigid habits. Maybe you'll discover you're a tightly wrapped person and you like to keep it that way. *Eventually,* one way or another, you'll hear time whisper powerfully about emptiness and aloneness, and about your tiny heart that didn't grow big enough to keep you or anyone else really warm.

You may accomplish a great deal but you'll achieve very little.

You'll die without much genuine love around you or in you.

You'll try to find ways to tolerate that void.

Superficial meanings once defended and sustained as deeply important will wither.

You'll grow more stale and moldy on the inside, maybe a little more groom and cologne on the outside.

You'll become, in your own way, desperate and critical; maybe a complainer, a whiner, a faultfinder, bitter and hardened: in retreat from daily reality as sunshine, smiles, and plans centered on acts of goodness with/for others.

One way or another you'll become a coward in denial and on the way out.

If you're in wedlock and neurotically compatible with a mate also in some form of adaptive denial, you'll both refute what I've just written as a non-applicable whatever—you'll acknowledge the dullness of your marital trance, shrug, and do what you do.

Man & male facts:

A man recognizes a male easily.

A male recognizes the presence of a man easily.

A man recognizes another man intuitively.

Men know that true love is *given,* that true love is *received,* and that true love has-to-be-*made.* This takes effort, openness, and a deeply generous heart.

Males offer, accept, and assemble possibilities (including persons) as things to be *used* and tolerated. That's the best that males aloof from deeper love can do. Males can be, however, helpful, nice, and friendly.

If you're *hardcore male,* your avoidance of self-honesty always leads to permanent arrogance. You'll never become a complete man no matter how hard you try with displays of money, influence, forceful attitude, and/or physical prowess. Those emphases will always reveal who you are, and they will tattoo you as 'fool'.

Only a fool believes he can fool others. The only person a fool can talk to for long is another fool.

Hardcore males are confined to superficial relationships based on convenience, desire, and shallow pleasures celebrated and repeated until boredom causes further restless love that becomes further fragmentation of self in a mood/attitude of *discontent* that doesn't go away. Ever.

Regular, everyday aging males who choose not to mature, slowly fade, then wade into the margins of personal nothingness leading to the shock of spiritual quicksand that keeps its promise: disappearance without bodily absence.

The point is: all aging males, hardcore or not, do their best to deny/hide personal pain. And to whatever extent the hiding works, it permits the continuity of a distorted personal agenda, because males usually try to find ways to make unacceptable behavior self-acceptable and *accepted*.

They never really, really say to themselves....

Then Keep It Real

Yes.

Keep it real means:

Learning how to relate to being alive positively, honestly, and creatively *all the time*. That's not a popular approach to living. It takes too much effort because—

It requires more respect for the specificity of words and the realities of meanings.

It requires learning that what you say always lands in another person's heart.

It requires more accurate reasoning instead of emotionalized logic.

It requires the willingness to seek more accurate insight.

It requires the avoidance of generalizing.

It requires thinking before speaking.

It requires humility and apologies.

It requires less defensiveness.

It requires more courage.
It requires availability
And change
For what's....

Related to keeping it real, I believe:

The development of courage is basic. Courage means being bigger than any hardship, anger, pain, frustration, fear, or *anxiety*. It's like being asked to put your arms around a Giant Sequoia Tree. The tree waits. You say I can't do this. The tree says you can. You say my arms aren't long enough. The Tree says do it. So you try. And you do it, barely. The Tree says now link your fingers. Your jaw drops. But you do it. The Tree says now hug. You do that. The Tree says now embrace me. You hesitate. Then you comply because you sense it *really matters*. The Tree says now stay in this embrace until you die. What do you say?

Adversity prepares us for the development of that kind of courage.

Without adversity you can't grow.

Without growth you won't love and your arms will embrace nothing.

Lies are the sand-structures of protected thought. They become the symptoms of self-waste that lead to the loss of personal power and further growth: call this disintegration, the beginning of structural collapse. What I'm describing is observable everywhere there are humans. Some folks just have more money to hide the madness.

The task of keeping it real is to make *living* try to match the goodness of *life*. And we're perfectly suited for doing that. But we all blow it to some extent because we start off 'blind'—in the hands of persons who keep us alive.

When we're young, we rely on others to teach us how to think and do. If what we're taught isn't reliable, *realistic* and/or truly applicable, we eventually learn that those persons who taught us couldn't really 'hear and see' very well or 'see' us accurately. They weren't really interested because of personal preoccupations due to unhappiness and low-key or overt craziness. They couldn't keep it real.

That's why most of us make the journey of aging inadequately equipped—we didn't learn how to 'see' more fully soon enough and then how to think more accurately soon enough so we could figure out how to keep it real *all the time*.

When we're young, we look *at* things. During our development, we begin to look *into* things and, eventually, for the possibility of joining, belonging, and finding a valid sense of personal purpose. If we find that purpose in a fairly balanced way, we begin to experience the essence of love in self and what keeping it real really means for the long haul.

The flipside:

Without valid and reliable 'sight', you can't develop the 'insights' necessary for the development of fully good *visions* of *reality, self,* and *the spiritual.*

Invalid or weak 'seeing' means you haven't learned *how* to think more *creatively* toward love and personal fulfillment: how to become a whole self instead of an individual at liberty and in discontent—troubled, conflicted, at odds, lost, in agony, miserable, blameful, resentful, vindictive, depressed, confused, anguished, or whatever word or phrase describes what about you is messed up.

All this, as you know, depends on what you learn to think and believe is *meaningful,* on what is valued and sought, on what to do and when, on who to hang out with, on what to want, buy, reject, accept, and on *how* you *learn* to *play* toward valid dreams.

'Growth' is the process that unites thinking, feeling, searching, discovering, aiming, risking, choosing, and learning, over and over. It includes self with self, self with others, and self creatively engaged in the truly worthwhile.

If education and training are deficient, growth won't happen adequately or regularly. You'll become a *version* of the true you: still functional but somehow missing out on solid growth.

But when you learn how to manage your freedom more accurately and wisely, you're happier, more creative, more realistic, and more lovable.

An early lesson in the management of freedom—keeping it real—is 'showing up' for every commitment: keeping your word to yourself and to others. Your word is your bond. Otherwise, you will deceive yourself and others until it no longer bothers you. That's weak and wrong. If you want living to improve, clean all that up....get real. Change.

Consider exploring the real by....

Naming your 'thought habits' and assessing which ones influence you for the good and the bad.

Listing your hot buttons, stubborn buttons, vulnerable buttons, I'm right buttons, control buttons, fear buttons, rigid buttons, lazy buttons, superiority buttons, and your double-standard buttons. Then try opening up to yourself honestly, then owning up to yourself actively by changing what has to be altered—seeing where in your world the tail wags the dog. Then train the dog. Change.

Studying yourself, the way you think, and why you think that way. Study your talents and others who excel in what attracts you, and study reality so you can figure out what 'living better' really means personally, socially, and spiritually.

If you think you're 'a work in progress', explain that in detail to someone: what the work is you're actually doing. Then point out proof of consistent progress that honestly reveals just how 'in' to the work you really are and just how far you've come since you started the work. Or is saying 'I'm a work in progress' just a verbal defense so you don't feel shame for being weak?

Remember, to pro-gress denotes that progress is active and measurable.

If you can't find a true man or a woman to help guide and mentor you, go to the library or a bookstore. Look for yourself among the books you like. Then decide if there's better stuff to read, better for you. If there is, find it and read it then go back to lesser books so you can begin to distinguish levels of quality, talent, skill, and content in contrast to *substance*—greater meanings—in the material and in you. Ask questions and answer them however you can.

Then go to museums, concerts, more bookstores, magazines stands, the mall, the street, the gutter, hospitals, and nature, and ask the same questions over and over. You'll get answers to whatever it is you really want to know.

If you don't get answers soon enough, you're not asking hard enough and waiting long enough. Keep asking. Keep doing. Keep seeking.

When you're in conversation, think about the person you're talking to and why they think the way they do. Develop the need to understand *what's really going on* in you, around you, in others, and *why*, and whether what you're doing is really good for you and will it take you where you need to go? Then answer the question 'where do I need to go and where do I want to go so I can feel like I'm getting somewhere that's not based on money, image, fantasy, and the fear of being left out?' All of this applies to all males of any age.

So....

Learning how to think more realistically to keep it *all real* is the basis of training for *strength* and the readiness to love: no illusions about yourself, others, your environment, the world, and beyond.

Strength, is the ability to perceive reality accurately and deal with it most effectively.

So....

Weakness is the flipside of that.

Which means....

Strength is learned.

Weakness is learned.

It's all in how you think, in the questions you ask, the answers you accept, and what you do. It's like a swimming pool: shallow end, middle, deep end.

Anyone who chooses the deep end dives in and tries to touch the bottom. Even in space.

Anyone who chooses the middle wants to float, paddle around, hang on to the edge of the pool, talk a lot, and sip iced tea.

Anyone who chooses the shallow end is scared.

Shallow living is coasting and watching. Which category are you in? Know anyone who's really asking the deep questions for real and going after answers?

More on the parental basics for keeping it real:

Valid parents provide valid stimuli for children, personally and environmentally. This facilitates the child's *fascination* in preparation for lasting *creative connections* of the dots to self: self to reality, self to one's inner 'world', self to environment, and, ultimately, self to realistic love in relationships and in community.

Ideally, this kind of parental facilitation and guidance becomes a pervasive appreciativeness *in* the child that is preparatory for optimism and confidence: can do, will do, gonna do, doing it and enjoying it.

If all that facilitation and guidance is not broken by trauma and mismanaged authority, then a child's inherently wonderful sense of enthusiasm and 'justice' will be manifest in the child's ability and capability to embrace the real that must be *preserved* in order to become increasingly 'realistic' and, therefore, more mature. The child slowly learns to reach for the possible and take the personal risks required for self-realization and valid love in relationship. That's the only way to truly become a cohesive self, a *person*. Otherwise, you're an individual with a name, shopping for who you are and displaying the results, positively or negatively. Along the way, you discover (or not) there aren't any stores that sell the answer.

So....

Valid parents *realistically, appropriately, consistently,* and *patiently* encourage and exemplify integrity and dignity through their concerns for education, unwavering receptivity, abundant curiosity, guided passion and desire, independence and interdependence, appreciation, self-discipline, striving, will, freedom and choice, good food, laughter, music, respect, courage, strength, fascination, friends, play, dreams, honest love, and earning enough money for living expenses, deeper pleasures, savings, and retirement.

Think about this:

After fifty years of living, options start to leave the party and you're left asking what party have I been attending all these years?

You begin to reassess. You hear time talking to you, and you think about the weight of wind telling you you're faced with 'getting older' and the end of your time: fewer dots to connect to fewer days.

The main dot left is the humble dot. It's connected to the love dot. If it's not, you're not humble. If you're not humble, your way of loving has been weak and, therefore, love in you and around you is less because of you.

Humble means no arrogance. None.

The love dot, humble dot, courage dot, strength dot, justice dot, compassion dot, joy dot, and all the other dots need lasting connectedness in you. If that doesn't happen, you're not keeping it real. And you won't fully mature.

So....

If you're willing to begin to see *beyond* the trance of naïve associations, narrow-minded ignorance, assumptions, opinions, anger, negative stubbornness, ideologies, arrogance, illusions, erroneous conclusions, convenient rationales, lies, and self-lies, you'll begin to *see into the basics of living* more completely: you were born, you have a few years, and you'll die with or without someone around who knows you or loves you.

Those you have truly loved will hold, and hold you.

They will not fail you or leave you.

They will 'live you' to the end of your time for as long as they live.

If you check out alone or with a few family members visiting once in a while, that will mean folks don't really care about you and you didn't do enough dot-connecting. You blew it. You never got the *point* of being alive. Love as a verb is the point, and it has to be actualized all the time from really good thinking and deciding, and *learning* that the *purpose* of living is defined by the quality of relationships you *forge* with self, others, and meanings.

Guaranteed: as you grow older, you will assess and reassess *love* and how you love or not, a little, or halfway. And you'll know, dimly or clearly, that faith is not belief. You'll know belief is related to faith the way fact is related to truth, the way stairs are related to height, and the way height is related to view.

If you're spiritually deluded, you'll believe against all that truth by imposing on truth what you'd like to believe. You won't have the courage to call it like it is, keep it real, and embrace the fullness of real truth, truth you're convinced you already know. You'll be defensively comfortable in your forms of daily anesthesia against growing pains.

But if you're willing to take the pains and get clear about what needs to be learned and done in your world, then go for it, do it now. Learn to be strong and realistic, able and willing to 'view' all the points in your world and the big-world points for exactly what they are. Then connect the truly true ones to reality realistically. That's how you develop viewpoints and a worldview that really matters.

Doing this implies the importance and growing presence of *vision*—how to see into you, into reality, and into the world....then how to find the best way to be you in the world so you're connected deeply to you, reality, others, and the big world.

For this to occur, we all need one or two great source teachers and abundant examples of great persons, great art, and great love because we need to learn, we need to love and be loved, and we need guidance and encouragement so we can, just like plants, eat 'light' and grow into what we already are.

Light for humans is called love.

Love is the deepest form of shelter, assertion, and affirmation. It has many shapes and sizes. Find yours, the one that fits, which means, you'll have to grow toward it and match its beauty through what you do for real: grow.

The love that fits you won't just happen 'from the universe' because no aspect of humanness is automatic, except potential and chemistry. The development and actualization of your potential, fairly or unfairly, is all on you.

If you genuinely seek light, it will find you.

How much of it do you want and how much of it can you take? That's a real self-conversation. Seeking light takes sustained effort, pure willingness to sustain that effort, and growing courage to *embrace* the entire task. And it requires dismissing all invalid viewpoints. That's where the rubber meets the road and folks back off and down.

It's the challenge most faiths avoid.

If you do go for it, you will learn that when you couldn't see the real dots you invented what you thought were valid dots and you connected to them.

You will learn that it takes time and effort to figure out how to drop old connections and make more valid connections to what truly matters most: 'seeing' better, thinking better, loving more completely, and doing what is most worthwhile with your time, talent, and money.

Conventionally, this is called maturing, growing up: learning to labor for love that includes wages and dreams.

A thought about laboring for love....

Loosely but specifically, valid seeking through doing can be called 'worship'.

Worship—going after the true truth, chasing it, finding it, and holding on to it while it grasps you into enthusiasm and reveals the best direction for your desire—will mature you in depth and scope because of the accuracy and expansion of your perspectives.

If that doesn't happen, worship gets lost in limiting rituals, senile traditions, emotion, false beliefs, ridiculous assumptions and conclusions, and in morbid resistance to wide open beauty and pleasure.

It ultimately gets lost in being scared by the simplicity and depth of big, mature worship—the wildly risky pursuit and expression of heaven through deep purpose related to the truly good. Worship then becomes a power-driven (not force) clarity of involvement that eliminates the numerous structures of rampant sham: zealotry, sentimentalism, combative intelligence, fear, self-congratulatory humility wrapped in false devotion, wrong self-sacrifice, and the presence of threat so subtly prevalent in most conventional and traditional worship and devotional practices.

So, yes....

Valid learning is the heartbeat of keeping it real: figuring out how to live in all ways so *love* can flourish in you and through you. This means love must be *made* realistically from its potential in each of us first, then toward others, the environment, and beyond.

Otherwise, there is silent tragedy—the loss of love. That's all around us and partly in us.

Timeline for keepin' it real:

In your *twenties*, what you really need and most deeply should be doing is the activity of 'gathering you'. You first. Do it. Then you'll be more ready to choose self-direction and include some company.

In your *thirties*, you take your availability and fullness into the world of deeper relationships and endeavor. You begin to *choose* more perceptively how and when your love can and should be made, and *why*; and you begin to discover just what the love really is that you say you are making or want to do.

This stage is the wonderful beginning of the *genesis risks* that require changing how you function.

Genesis risk is *the* supreme challenge for the rest of your life because it signifies the personal outcry for more meaningful creativity that will morph you toward and into the clarity of your *purpose* on this planet. It includes the kind of work you do, the kind of fun you have, how you choose to seek full mental and physical health, who you hang with, selecting a mate very realistically, what you do with money, and how you choose what's most valuable to cherish, nurture, and protect. It all adds up slowly to what you are 'making' of yourself and what you will have 'made'—*really done*—when you hit my age.

In your *forties,* time says 'build' more, structurally and personally, and be open to spiritual upheaval that will make you run gauntlet harder but sharper.

In your *fifties,* time says 'okay, this is what you've done, so now look ahead at your sixties. Check out the numbers and be ready to acknowledge that your youth ended twenty years ago, you're in the middle of middle age, and what's really up is: getting old. Talk to older folks. They'll usually give it to you straight'.

In your *sixties,* time will talk to you more regularly and you won't talk back. Instead, you'll self-talk about what you've really *done,* what you really *know,* and what you'll *do* for the rest of your time before you get a disease, a stroke, a heart attack, or just plain die.

If you listen closely and understand time's dialect real well when it talks about the now, you'll quickly understand that there are no 'golden years'. But there is abundant beauty. That's the gold.

If you can really integrate the now deeply, you'll automatically move toward giving, toward courage and the affirmation of deeper love, and toward a simpler surrender.

If you don't hit your fifties and sixties in stride with your years, then you're in position to acknowledge that you didn't keep up because you didn't keep it real. You're outta step with it all....troubled, troubling, and troublesome. Ever know a real cranky old person, someone who's just not nice? They missed the boat and they know it.

But when you're younger and figuring out how to put something together for real, you have the luxurious opportunity to choose the hardship-goodness experiences of genesis risk. If you jump on that opportunity, you'll be in place to develop more courage, strength, and insights to help you really start lining up with the true facts and greater and greater meanings that will sustain you during the rigors of the next few decades. You'll begin to sense your personal *valor* and *virtue,* two words packed with meanings greater than conventionally assumed.

And, if you're alert and willing right to the end, you'll die shifting gears and accelerating all the way into liftoff.

In your *seventies and eighties*: make sure you've got enough good memories, photographs, 'family', and cash so you can stay airborne and keep smilin' till the end of the ride.

On a personal note:

The qualifications I listed for being able to write this book indicate a lot of experiences. But I never hit low points that made me ask what's the point? I sensed the point was to *live*. Do it. And that point has always been alive in me in a really good way. I'm glad. Made me want to learn. Survive. Do. Risk. Keep on truckin'.

About twenty years ago, my daughter, Sadie, commented on the autobiography I'd just begun. She said, 'Pa, you're just a middle-class, laid back professor so why would anyone want to read about your life?' I told her, 'Well, it's been an endless rodeo that includes events I never entered but had to do anyway. That means, in a general way, about the only thing I haven't seen or been through is murder. That's a whole bunch of autobiography.' She looked at me from her teenage mind and paused. Didn't say anything.

There *are* a lot of stories, and it's fun to tell them spontaneously. But I'm reluctant to write about me in this book because what's really important is sharing what I learn. That's why I became a teacher.

Students often asked if we could skip the assignment and so I could tell stories about my life. Sometimes I said okay. My son-in-law recently told me 'Ya gotta put some of yer stories in the book so readers can relate.' Sadie co-signed that. I said okay.

So, okay:

What have I seen and done? Some of it no one needs to know.

The stories go from ugly-ugly to sublime.

So, okay, here are some of the real-points, good stuff points, tough points, some cry points, but never give up or die from it all points, just keep rollin' points....

◆ I grew up on the lip of an active volcano that erupted all the time as alcohol, gunshots, screaming, gritty sexuality, arguing, beatings, threats, hunting, and dogs killed for no reason. My father was crazy but bright. A 30-06, a .12 gauge pump-action, a machete, a quirt, boards, his belt, fists, mouth, and eyes. He used it all.

◆ My mother whored discreetly. Forty bucks a pop. My father hid and watched. She did our German Shepherd. Did local guys. Did things. Worked at a job. Worked hard. Was liked. Pretty. Popular. Outgoing and friendly. When I was fifteen, she showed me 8x10 glossies of her in action. Then she cried and asked me what to do.

✦ I knew everything about both of them year after year.

✦ I started working when I was 10. Up at 4 a.m. to ride with Kit Carson, the bread man, making deliveries.

✦ Often, I was afraid to go home when I was in elementary school. But I went anyway. Then I got a job selling newspapers after school in bars and stores. In summers I mowed lawns.

✦ Then became a teenager and worked more. I had to sleep at the house. My father kicked my brother out; my sis went to live with a friend.

Argue argue argue....my mother mostly just listened, stone-faced, to the verbally abusive rape of her character. Then they brought it all to me for sympathy.

I wanted the house to be a home but it felt like a sealed tomb in prayer for sunlight. So home didn't happen. But I still wanted to help my parents because I was a kid who always wanted to help.

✦ In high school I played sports, rode horses, worked year round, dated, went 'steady', was popular, tried to fit in, dug cars and pickups, and started to write what I hoped was poetry. But I was convinced I wasn't all that bright.

✦ One early evening in late August just before I was a senior, I was swimming laps in the local pool that had been open for a few years. I was the lifeguard. The weather was cold and gray. When I got out, two guys were standing near the fence. They motioned me over. I told them the pool was almost closed. They didn't care. They said they'd just graduated from the U. of Minnesota and were on their way to the west coast. Swimmers. They asked my name. I told them and said I wasn't part of a team and that I usually swam in a lake not far from town. That fall I received a letter from the swimming coach at the U of M. inviting me to visit the campus. I did. Swam for him. Was offered a partial scholarship. I went. Worked as a janitor cleaning dorm toilets, worked at the pool, worked, and met the challenge of training 100 percent. Then I had a major-major disappointment at the Frosh-Varsity swim meet. That was real tough. At the end of the year I was in deep question so....

✦ I quit school in June. Got a ride to San Francisco. Got a ride to LA. Went to Burbank and sat on a curb near the airport in first-time smog, and wondered whether I'd be able to board a non-scheduled airlines flight to Hawaii. I did:

a converted WWII prop plane. Took eleven hours; loose rivets, surfboards under the seats, and one stewardess. Got to Honolulu, had a run in with the Metropolitan Police (giant Samoans), and later sneaked into a hotel by climbing over a lower-room balcony. Got a job working on the construction of the International Airport. There's more to this story.

+ Fell in love-crush at a dance.

+ Left Hawaii. Went to southern California and stayed till Christmas. Went back to college because I understood I'd be doing odd jobs and menial labor forever if I didn't give my mind what it needed. I really met my mind and it said 'study'.

+ No money. Poor. But I still hitchhiked, had to go and see whatever I could....one time to Manhattan. Spring of '63. Long haul. Pulled into NYC at dawn, buildings magically silhouetted. I wanted to be a great actor so I had to see plays in New York so I had to hitchhike, so I did, and saw some bad plays, stayed at the Y, got lost in Harlem....there's more to this story.

+ Finished college in August of '65. Went to graduation with an infected wisdom tooth pocket. No cards. No family. Graduated. Got a ride west.

Said goodbye to family, left Newport Beach—
my father took me to the highway and said 'if
you get out of this car, you'll be responsible for
my death'. I remember opening the door as a
natural act of courage, and closing it. I had to do
what I did. It was mine to do and it was good,
a good dream I was determined to make come
true. He sped off, spit road gravel; I looked at
the red Buick disappear….and raised my arm,
thumb out. Hitched to NYC. A midnight ride,
last ride on the Cyclone rollercoaster. Slept with
a girl. Boarded a freighter the next morning….
bound for Europe with a hundred bucks in my
wallet and no way home. I'd been drafted for
Vietnam and reclassified due to injuries. There's
more to that story.

✦ Stood next to a kid in a dark trench coat, long
wavy hair…sailed past the Statue of Liberty.
I said 'Hi, I'm Jim Wilson.' 'Mario Savio.' I
didn't know he was leader of the Free Speech
Movement in Berkeley. He told me the FBI
was on his ass. He was down, preoccupied. We
talked. Eleven days later, after a mid-Atlantic
storm (there's a great story about that—I looped
my belt on a steel post on the prow and rode
bronc-style, screaming my delight up toward
twilight clouds and deep down into the maw of

black waves), we arrived in Holland, and France, finally, at Southampton....

✦ The stories are too numerous but I did it all, did it the hard way. It didn't feel that hard because I was too excited about studying in London for three years. There's a beautiful story attached to how that happened. A first class miracle, just like the swimmers and other events of 'luck': beyond mere chance.

✦ Hitchhiked across Europe three times, went into North Africa, got jumped by three guys in a narrow street late at night after I tried to hustle a dancer who turned out to be a guy (there's more to this story), rode a motorcycle nonstop from Algeciras to London, took a wild plane ride, did Ireland all the way to loving Ireland, slept under cars on lower levels of ships in the Mediterranean, jumped on and off trains, had a run-in with the law about that on a train leaving Berlin, fell in love in Nice, saw so much art, studied, and learned....did Sicily....met a midnight whore on the docks of Marseilles (a strangely sad and beautiful moment), got picked up by Mafiosi in Sardinia and did a Hollywood roll out of their black Mercedes on a slow curve, then (this is a great moment) walked the hills all

night on a moonlit path leading to San Teresa
Gallura; found Easter Sunday at the Vatican,
wept openly five feet from the Pieta, hitchhiked
more and never got sick but once in Switzerland,
saw hardcore drug parties in London, never did
drugs or alcohol....did intercourse, searched,
studied, and became an actor.

+ When I was 21, just before Europe, I made a
  vow to work out until the day I died. Always
  carried five cords and two handles when I traveled. Kept that vow even in a hospital bed the
  day after two major surgeries. Used cords.

Still work out, no matter what.

I love really good food, organic stuff, and it's not
easy to get in rural Wyoming—140 miles roundtrip.
But I get as much as I can because I *identify* with body,
health, and food.

I know the flipside—

My original family all died from craziness: alcohol,
cigarettes, self-abuse, and neurosis never conquered.
I watched it happen, up close and personal. Did all I
could. I learned that if anything isn't good for my body
or mind, I didn't want it. That approach narrowed my
socializing options....

+ On and on, so many stories....at 25 I came
  back to America....two weeks later, I landed

a top NY agent and a *small* role in Midnight Cowboy....stood next to a short, dirty guy on set...introduced himself as Dustin Hoffman. 'Jim Wilson.' We talked about boxing. I didn't know who he was. I was cut from the film. I didn't care.

+ Went to Broadway as an understudy.

+ Went to Los Angeles. Went through a classic Hollywood event because of a major movie star.

+ Proposed to the girl I'd met in Hawaii (there's a lot more to all this) by putting a wedding band in a roast beef sandwich and meeting her during her lunch hour at the beach.

+ Motorcycles, hotrods, books, arrested in Tijuana, strip search, became a father (yay!), quit acting, went searching for me again, found me, and kept on rolling into the beauty and thunder of it all.

+ Became a teacher and tried to keep on learning how to write a sentence.

+ Went back to school. Got another degree.

+ Went to Reed College to teach.

+ Went to Cornell University to teach. Became a father again. Yay!

+ Dropped the professorship at Cornell and went to USC for pennies as a Lecturer because I was trying to save a marriage. Couldn't save it. Working my ass off to pay bills. Three jobs. I'm not afraid of work. Never was. When I was little, a cowboy told me 'git that done, you cain't drown in yer own sweat'. He was right.

◆ And the beat goes on through stories that include triumph, defeat, shame, regret, heartbreak, the stupids, growth, and love….until, after over 30 years in the saddle, I retired from USC classrooms, stopped coaching and teaching classroom to a-list actors, and returned to Wyoming where, on these thirty-five acres in a valley on the west slope of mountains near the Montana border, I now live in a 100 year-old log cabin I bought for $400 and moved it to this bald knoll with a great view. And here I am. Spent my first year and a half with critters, a space heater, a dog, and the thrill of change I call adventure….and more stories.

All of my experiences point from this book to you. By that I mean—

I hope you can sense that going for it, whatever that means to you, won't fail if what you're going for is the real deal for you right now, something that will lead you into your kind of creativity for the long haul. So just do it. Take the risks to get answers. No bullshit, no fear, no holding back. Take the steps, take the hits and keep rolling. And when you get down, scared, insecure, doubtful, or in need of assistance, look at the end of your arm. It's the best place, as Oscar Wilde wrote, to find a helping hand. Get busy. Move that hand to tasks, the ones that'll move you forward until your heart and mission join up again. If all that's a true match, the dream will, one way or another, come true. Be strong, courageous, and willing to work relentlessly into the wild pleasure of accurate *pursuit* while still including your friends and the folks you-say-you-love.

So, thank you and back to this book....

Man and male facts:

A man lives in the realities of greater meanings and defends those meanings fleibly.

A male lives in the realities of lesser meanings and defends himself rigidly or shifts meanings around to secure the acceptance and advancement of a narrow personal agenda.

A male does versions of the good and emphasizes pleasure and/or repetitive 'winning'.

Winning can prepare a male for the tasks of becoming a man but it can also wear him out by seducing him over and over until he's a fool for what's no longer relevant. Then he becomes irrelevant to himself; he just can't see that fact but he can feel it.

A worn-out, aging male has nowhere to turn, nowhere to go. But he has to come up with something to somehow feel *engaged*. So he usually tries repeating what worked before….until he gets the point too late and realizes he's been on a personal merry-go-round of nothing connected to the new: no self-renewal (growth) and very little maturing. This takes him to a dead-end address called alone, with or without company and money. In the center of alone is a mirror: time for deep talk instead of grooming.

If you're a worn-out male who doesn't want to have that talk, your boredom will mature and take you with it.

Mature boredom is a permanently lukewarm bath without soap.

However....

If you're a young male, please understand that boredom is partially normal; it's a condition of readiness for deeper creativity—learning how to make things happen for *you*.

Flipside....

If you're not *willing* to learn and change, you're partially blind and in a state of self-waste. That's tragic.

Self-waste can be turned around but it takes *courage* and *strength*—learning how to think better, changing what has to be changed, and acting wisely so you can be a more complete you. To do that, you first have to be brave—*willing* to be present to listen fully to reality's quiet lecture about you.

Facts:

The powerful union of will to strength and bravery to courage is the essence of 'hero'.

Courage under pressure, then under extreme pressure, means *do not wither*.

All men are hero. All women are hero.

Men and women do not wither. Ever. They know that courage, strength, bravery, will, pain, struggle, thinking, actions, and unwavering dedication must be united positively, realistically, and wisely all the time.

They know the purpose of living is to mature by enhancing the presence of love, beginning with self and always extended to children.

Male cowardice facts....

Cowardliness in young males is part of the package of being young and unformed, uninformed, and, therefore, immature. It's a vacancy, a void to be filled. But it's not a negative.

Trench-cowards calculate and manipulate to avoid deeper engagement with self, others, and reality. They're defensive. That's a negative.

Cowardly, aging males usually are stubborn and intolerant....or both, *and* arrogant. Often, they're unlikable and unlovable, and eventually excluded even though they might be a friend, spouse, neighbor, relative, co-worker, or colleague.

America is a nation of too few men. That fact unites America with all other nations. Many males. Few men. Why? Young males accept aging males' false versions of manhood and become aging males. That's why.

Young males cannot define a man or easily find one. No one around them can either.

Integrity....

Abstractly:

It's a concept.

It's an aspect of justice.

It's an aspect of power.

It's a declaration of the will to love fully.

Concretely, integrity is *balanced continuity*—the unbroken *integration of all structures and stimuli* in the evolving situations and conditions called being alive.

Continuity of balance requires flexibility, adaptability, and a full willingness to seek the possible while maintaining a deep respect for reality and relationships.

You can't put your spin on integrity. Either you're in for the truly good or you're in for your preferred version of the truly good, or you're not really in at all.

So....

Integrity is the most realistic basis for all aspects and forms of progress.

It's the core of all moral experience.

It's the means for expressing vitality—the drive of life in the activity called living. Depth of vitality means the extent that your integrity is creative and truly positive.

Integrity reveals the best of what the word passion means when related to truth. Passion and truth united are present in great persons, anonymous or famous.

The development of integrity secures *dignity*: respect.

The applications of integrity and dignity is called humility: the authentic drive to *encounter* the humanity of another person, the wild beauties of nature and earth, and the holiness of existence known to us in our version of being called human. No arrogance.

On dignity....

Most broadly, dignity is sustained, active respect for all that is and isn't, from the ground up, into space, and beyond space.

Most immediately, dignity is related to *seeing* and *honoring* all forms of being then respectfully connecting dots to *preserve* the integrity of all forms of being. This applies to everyone you know, everyone you meet, all creatures, all things, all that you do and make, and all that made you.

A perspective:

Reduced integrity and/or dignity cause conflict.

Continued reduction of integrity or dignity intensifies conflict.

If conflict continues unresolved, disintegration toward *chaos* occurs.

Any motion toward chaos expands fear. That can break you into your anxiety—motion toward self-*absence*.

Usually, the response to the threat of self-absence is the drive to annihilate the threat. That either takes the form of action done with complete determination experienced as the positive use of will and the clear guidance of desire....or, tragically, you go the other way only to discover *there is no other way*, no way out except the no-way-out mega-tantrum actions of destructiveness, violence, suicide, or some kind of long and bad personal war that can ruin you and the lives of others.

Keeping it real through play....

Play, as you know, is basic to how we discover.

Discovery, as you know, facilitates the development of thought, language, meanings, and *expression*.

Expression is action done to secure objectives that conclude in positive or negative goals.

Positive play unites self, reality, meaning, facts, power, freedom, and responsible.

Negative activity unites reality, meaning, facts, force, freedom, and irresponsible.

Sometimes, we're afraid to play and we need encouragement to play again and again so we discover how to play for keeps. This book is all about that kind of encouragement.

We admire folks who put it out there, put it all on the line, deal with realities and reach for the dream because that's what we're *all* supposed to do. That's what freedom ultimately is—going the distance of personal growth until you glimpse fulfillment and some holy.

Children play sincerely—completely, from the inside out. They're never serious. But they are enviably sincere. And, as you know, a child playing is *in* activity toward more complex forms of play that eventually include the awareness of how time, meanings, and structures can be coordinated most effectively and creatively—expressively.

Play is the only innocence we can know. Innocence means womb.

Womb is about impregnation for birth as the renewal of life.

Play is how we honor the word 'life' as the power of what is, what is possible, and what must be saved. If you're not trying to make great play and love, and helping others do that, you're probably just trying to make money, make do, and feel special somehow.

Play or die. Love or die.

Therefore, play. And love to live through love.

Man-cry:

The battle cry of a man will intimidate and amaze because it's made without sound.

The battle cry of a man is in his eyes: wholly ready for action or wholly in action for the holy. It's a cry against all that would negate love.

Applying this info....

If you're going to keep it real toward no illusions, you quickly learn that personal pain is the hardest classroom because the lectures really hurt, they're really scary, and they really put you on the spot: you have to decide to stay enrolled or ditch.

In order to stay enrolled, you have to be willing to learn how to think in ways that make staying justified and *desirable*.

Men stay enrolled for a lifetime and do the lessons over and over, take the exams over and over. That means they study. Every day. They take on the challenges and they take the hits. They know the hits will heal because pain is just pain. It's hard to live into that fact, that reality, that yes.

Man/woman facts:

Men and women know that any reduction of personal integrity and dignity is a loss of love to the world. They also know reduced integrity and reduced dignity is the way of the world.

No male or female is hero but both can be heroic. An act of bravery and devotion can be heroic but the doer is not hero. Hero for the purpose of this book is determined by the duration of heroic: a way of living.

Only a man or a woman is hero. It's a daily activity called deeply normal engagement in realities. And the aim of that engagement is to produce love by doing the good for self and others genuinely.

A man and woman know ignorance and arrogance are pedestals of isolation tragically protected by the unreasonable reasoning of the ignorant and the arrogant. A man and woman know how ignorance, arrogance, and defensive insecurity cause an intense conviction that one is 'right'.

No man or woman ever claims to be right. They struggle to remain 'in the right'.

The shift from being 'right' to deciding for the truly right comes from the humility dot—the 'voice and action' for dignity and compassion.

Again, humility means no arrogance. *None.*

Men and women know that any departure from the truly good initiates arrogance. Arrogant persons find ways to argue against that fact because arrogant persons are arrogant. Arguing is partly how they try to stay balanced on stilts.

Men and women know that humility, dignity, and compassion inevitably produce genuine giving, and that *giving* is the center of one's humanity.

Giving cannot be confined to time, things, and cash. It's also the quality of pervasive openness to the new—the willingness to reinterpret living *honestly* and *receptively*.

Few persons go all out that way, go the distance, answer the call fully, take the risks, and really put it all on the line, genuinely and knowingly, for love.

Men go all out.
Males go out.

Men line up.
Males use lines.

Any approach to living that isn't oriented toward deep giving is sentimental extravagance, manipulation, the pouring of cynical acid on the cloths of heaven, or making spiritual manure and marketing it.

A thought about that
kind of marketing....

Thousands of religious leaders and politicians with local, national, or international influence are afflicted with aberrant thinking carefully structured for appeal to persons they know will agree.

They pimp ideas. They hustle.

They plan and rehearse their assertions.

They perform.

They make manure, offer it for sale, and collect.

At this point, you might want to ask....

Why write all this? Why not just say it in a nutshell, Wilson, and be done?

The topic of this book, becoming a man, is a tough nut to crack. And writing about the nut rather than the shell is more complex than simple. We'll get crackin' later.

If the problems caused by aging males running the planet, corporations, and homes weren't a reality, then becoming a complete man wouldn't be so problematic and I wouldn't be writing this book. But most males, irrespective of age, education, status, or wealth *can't really answer the question* 'What is a man?' Physical size, age, a beard, intercourse, keeping a job, paying bills on time, military service, taking care of business, experiencing a wedding ceremony or not, and generating family are the usual references cited as adequate evidence of being a man.

And that's valid until you ask the question 'Do you do it all with *mature love* all the time?' For males, the answer must be no.

A perspective....

Many young to aging males typically seek a strong, maternal female who's fun, attractive, and really nice and supportive, and flexibly willing to tolerate male immaturity as lovable and forgivable *for the long haul*; no questions, no fighting, no pushiness, and not too much demand on male time so he can 'do his thing'.

Or they look for a beautiful female or for one who will take over and lead the way.

Or they don't know what they want because they're resigned to thinking that 'love relationships basically are over'. So they quit looking....but they don't forget.

Other males resist the questions of manhood and maturity, and accept passivity, loneliness, possessions, and bacon bits called porn.

Or males just want sex, no real commitments, and no hassle: uncomplicated companionship, availability, and compliance; low maintenance or no maintenance.

Or some males are fools for what they think love is because of what they need it to be. So they're easily blinded.

No male seeks a woman because he knows she would not choose him. He may, however, intuitively seek a potential woman because he somehow senses there is a difference between a female and a woman.

Consider:

Lovers of love don't engage in false love.
Men are lovers of love.
Women are lovers of love.
Therefore, they love into....

Beauty:

Beauty is the *actual presence* of greater meanings experienced as truth: love in motion. That means the motion of beauty is *perfect motion*. And we respond to it because we can, because that perfection is in each of us already. So we live the beauty and cherish the moment. And we want to keep it yet somehow share it.

We rely on beauty for memories, joy, healing, and hope.

The deep experience of beauty and truth makes us weak for love.

No man is weak for love until love and desire *win* him to a beloved.

AND CRACK THE NUT: VISION

CRACKING THE NUT means changing how you think, putting it all together for the new, and then putting it all on the line for personal progress: doing it, for real.

Before you get crackin', you have to really *want* to do it because it's not easy. But it's worth it. To be really motivated requires that you can truly 'see' the value of changing. Then you either take the risk and make it happen, procrastinate, or shift into neutral and coast downhill.

Vision requires accurate perceptions of *reality, self,* and *spirit* that must be unified and sustained. What does that mean? It means you put all three together personally, realistically, and meaningfully then you live that way, honestly and openly.

Vision of Reality:

A vision of reality results from what you've learned, how you learned it, how you evaluate what you've learned, and how you change to make living better—more realistic.

Consider:

When great persons restore our 'sight', we feel admiration, gratitude, respect, and hope as renewals of security, will, and optimism. Their words, actions, and work—their visions—help us to reinforce truth as reality, reality as truth, and both as the basis for superior experiences of beauty. They inspire us. They make some 'light' so we can sense our truest nature and go for it more through what we do. We need those beacon folks so we can clarify the relationship of self to self and to the profundities of the simple that surround us as the obvious.

Further consider:

All humans draw conclusions about self, reality, living, and relationships. Either these conclusions are accurate, erroneous, or a mixture of both.

Most conclusions include un-discussed assumptions that remain unquestioned.

Eventually, however, reality *weighs in* for full attention. You're either straight up honest about it and deal with it, or you deny it, or you lie.

Denial and the lie pervade nearly all reasoning, beliefs, and actions personally, nationally, and globally because of fear, the fear of loss.

Most folks seek just enough vision of reality and true facts to establish adequate functioning, financial security, some 'fun', a way to belong, and a sense of personal purpose.

Bottom line:

You will do what is important to you even though it might not be what's most important to do.

This fact tells you about your vision of reality— what it is, what it could be, what you are, what you could be, what you don't question, what you need to ask, and what you do question but don't really answer.

Personal vision of reality always includes a worldview—your basic attitude—about the big world of reality.

Examples of worldviews:

Life sucks; It's a war zone; Do what ya gotta do 'cause no one's gonna do it for you; Go for it; Count your blessings; Trust in the Lord; Everything happens for a reason but I don't understand the reasons; It's God's plan; It's all relative; F-it, we're just gonna die anyway so I'm in it for me; Reach for the stars; Dreams can come true; It's all about money; It's all a game, etc....

Whatever your vision of self in reality is, it matters. If it's distorted, change it. Get help....crack the nut—*crack you*: crack from uptight, from too loose, from too conservative, from too liberal, from too idealistic, from too narrow, from too naïve, from too sentimental, from too bitter and hard, from negative judgments, from arrogance, from too aloof, from stingy and cheap, from controlling, from too scared, from manipulative, from defensive, from lazy, from complacent, from distracted, from anger, from the need to escape, from evasive, from procrastination, from impatient, from critical....

Find yourself in those examples then talk to someone.

Then consider listing all nouns in your world that are really important to you.

List them in order of priority. Look at the priorities you honor daily. They'll tell you who you are, what you avoid, and what you need to avoid and include; they'll form the basis for more 'dot-connecting' related to how you link thought, feeling, belief, and action to the structures of daily living. They'll help you understand the how and why of your opinions, attitudes, judgments, approaches, assumptions, conclusions, viewpoints, biases, discriminations, hopes, fears, goals, and actions, and, therefore, how you cope with reality.

Decide what you need to change. Then open up and get crackin'.

Cracking against the familiar for the new is hard. It feels risky because it is.

With that in mind, think about....

Going into deep mountain wildness for a few weeks on foot.

What happens when you enter?

For those of you who've gone into wild nature for any meaningful length of time, you know nature becomes a highly concentrated presence that doesn't include or exclude you; you know you're just another creature centered on *survival*. Immediately, you become highly aware of how you think and how you *choose*. That's a very intimate insight regarding vision of self as a creature that is significant and *insignificant*: relevant but irrelevant—relevant to you but irrelevant to all else around you, unless you're perceived as a threat.

You quickly understand that you're just another anonymous form of life gripped by the need for food, shelter, and *safety*. Your appearance, name, income, social status, history, race, personal life, and non-wild opinions aren't important because you have *no influence* over any thing around you. All you have is your freedom to choose how to coordinate with the realities you-are-in. Your choices boil down to discovering ways to survive, step by step, because no step in wild nature can be taken for granted. Your entire being must engage with reality constantly to ensure complete reception of all stimuli pertinent to survival and advancement toward destination.

Your vision of reality becomes *now* related to *next*. Now, next, you, and nature must unite through perception and action, step after step. Amazingly, you will always look out and up; you will look and *see* more deeply into the 'now' with awe, appreciation, uncertainty, thoughtfulness, and fear....you will look into nature and see living conclusions of truth and beauty somehow present in the inexplicable but obvious miracle of the purely natural. And that makes you different than any other creature—because you can think and wonder about it all.

But....

If natural purity of environment is not a valued personal symbol, you'll feel/think you have nothing in common with anything around you; and if you're anxiety prone, you'll see nature as terrain that isn't landscaped. It's not tame. It's threatening: filled with bugs, spiders, animals, poisonous plants, impure water, no facilities, no direction except by compass, stars, and sounds. There won't be anything about nature to appreciate because it's in your face and it's unpredictable, undeniably permanent, and *still*. And something in it can kill you. If you can't get in your car and say 'I'm outta here', you're left with two choices—learn and go on or stay still and perish; action or inertia.

To learn means you have to *see* differently by really seeing the dots—you have to see *into* environment as *the* place of profoundly interconnected interdependencies. Then you have to accurately start connecting the dots of structures and conditions affecting your survival.... because time's importance is its immediacy related to accurate choices, food, water, and getting some rest. You learn that time intensely includes the future *because* of the now. The past becomes nearly irrelevant.

Guaranteed: If you stay a while in wild nature, you will smile often. You will celebrate into moments of joy. You will learn about 'spirit' and the 'spiritual' in the real because nothing is abstract in wild nature, ever. It might be unfamiliar but it isn't abstract. That's the draw of its deep integrity pumping and present around you. And because of your arousal toward wild nature, the essentials in it and in you are intensified, simplified, and clarified *as a union* that feels like thought following light.

That kind of insight is transcendent because it transcends you and includes you: you have a relationship with what omnipresent love most deeply is as wild beauty and your wild beauty. You get way closer to 'in'. You start to crack the nut. The nut is always you.

So....

If you *study* reflectively on the wholeness of nature as *your* wild beauty also, you'll be more aware of reality every time you make the journey into that form of holiness called human. Wild beauty will teach you how to see self, reality, and others more clearly, openly, and compassionately. You'll be more able to read reality for the 'what's next' challenge of your world and relationships. And it will always boil down to 'the next step' and how to take it. You'll choose and move accurately. When you can do that, you're crackin' the nut even more: learning how to think better and keep it really real, closer to 'in'. When you're finally 'in', you feel balanced, anchored, centered.

If you're a wild beauty novice, it's better to have a teacher with you so you can appreciatively learn:

To walk, wishing your feet made no mark on virgin soil;

To understand sanctity and the joy of paradise revisited;

To understand the significance of the word blight and....

To acknowledge wild beauty in what is casually called space.

The wild in us is the basis for our morality. And the first lesson in morality is to learn how to get out of the way of the real. Be *receptive*. Then line up with reality. The wild beauty of all the naturals and all its creatures can teach you how to do that more than any person. A person can only help translate your perceptions into a more valid vision of reality—one that always includes beauty as truth, truth as beauty. If these two inseparable facts are deeply experienced and held, you're more ready to explore the essential in contrast to the necessary, the real in contrast to the invented, and the possible related to the new. You'll be developing courage.

Yes,

Love is the ultimate wild beauty. And when you're in it you can't speak because there aren't words for it. You can only do what it is. And smile a lot until you cry.

Facts forward:

Our species is evolving into another era of profound change. We're unprepared for the responsibilities of what many reluctantly call our progress.

We are being pushed by our inventions into a deeper wildness of truth, love, beauty, courage, and responsibility.

We are learning that what we create we must live with, live for, or die from. That's a major stimulus for major anxiety and major courage.

Our species still has enormous difficulty connecting the dots of self, reality, and meanings.

The more humans subdue wild nature through alteration without remorse or regret, and eliminate valid aspects of greater religion without remorse or regret, the more *things* humans will invent to secure 'distance' from wild nature, wild beauty, persons, and greater meanings. That's the route of major cowardice and destructiveness. And it's happening today, big time.

Vision of Self:

Vision or version?
Vision or image?
Authentic or borrowed?
Reality or trance?

A realistic vision of self requires that you learn how to be realistic about you, love, doing, and dying. This means you must consider your willingness to grow.

Growth is *the* personal 'immaculate conception'. It is actualization toward full self-humanity and it is motion toward other-humanity—goodness leading to the *birth of love* in self and for others. The birth of love personally and interpersonally reveals the fullest meaning of power as the awareness *of,* the manifestation *of,* and participation *in* the greatest of meanings.

Vision of self facts:

We're basically on our own and we know it.

We live in an increasingly anxious period of cultural eruptions.

We *make homes* on a planet spinning in space that's mostly *dark, silent, airless,* and completely impersonal.

We attempt to avoid the implications of these raw facts by inventing explanations that prevent courageous thinking and answering the question....what's next for *all* of us?

Morality is the centrality of goodness perceived, received, integrated, done, and sustained: whatever is best must be done, what is done must be best. That's the only law of love in morality. We all transgress that law.

To the extent that love is reduced or absent, tragedy occurs—very real losses of the valuable. This is reversible until it's too late.

Expecting young persons to be mature under age thirty-five is ignorant, unrealistic, and harshly negative.

Much thinking in politics and a great deal of teaching in the area of religion is guided by narrow minds and small hearts connected to language/doctrine/ideology that cements mind and heart into bunkers of protective viewpoints disguised as generous and defended as 'right'. This enhances personal and cultural bastions of absurd reasoning while increasing the volatile frenzy of static vision.

As suggested, an accurate vision of self requires that you see into the actual 'you' to be developed into the 'me I know I *am*' rather than that lingering mix of:

Authentic.	Artificial.
Genuine.	Costume.
Courage.	Coward.
Mature.	Immature.

You experience matrimony or not, have a child or children, or not; get sick, see others get sick, see others die and, perhaps, die earlier than expected; you make more or less money, spend wisely or not, or hoard; you pay bills, become humble, more generous and compassionate, or more bitter and stingy, or somewhere in the middle.

You arrange objects, bathe, have accidents, forget to do things, exercise or not, have fantasies, compare self to others, and observe the changes in your body.

You bleed, acknowledge weather, spend money, eat, do laundry, kill insects, decorate, socialize, rearrange objects, criticize, gossip, yearn, have numerous doubts, and experience illness/disease. You age. And during aging, you acknowledge currently and in retrospect a series of 'last time' events....until the last of the last times becomes your last now.

In various ways you learn to prevent stupid choices by answering *the basic questions* that contribute to whether you become a more complete man or remain a male, become a more complete woman or remain a female.

Men seek maturity and deeper success.

Males tend to seek money, possessions, and some kind of style. Or they don't care much about success because the word is a depressing reminder.

Men serve; males like to be served.

Male conformists like to be praised; male non-conformists like to 'rebel'. American admiration of 'rebels' reinforces rebellion beyond adolescence; personal rebellion beyond adolescence is rarely admirable or valuable.

The only valid rebellion is creativity for the continuity of goodness.

Wealth denotes an aspect of mature success if it's given away genuinely and wisely.

Reality does not respond to human pressure. Reality lets the false die. Only a human will hold on to the false. This is the basis of the unrealistic visions that govern the planet.

Greatness of person is always noticeable by the absence of self-announcement. Folks in the presence of a great person experience admiration and the desire to praise and know the person, if only for a moment.... touch some human light.

Greatness of person is not necessarily linked to formal education. Many great persons aren't 'smart' (deeply informed) but their substance is brilliant, deeply bright; the 'light' of their brightness and what they do with it shines and it is *heard* by all willing to see it. It's inspirational: living proof of immaturity transcended....a person who is free within the holiness of freedom and doing the work of freedom as the holy: working for the good.

Aging males and females didn't fully learn how good living can be and how it's done.

Old males and females missed out on too much.... it shows in their words, actions, and eyes, eyes that talk of living where less love dwells.

Men and women *feel* fear, pain, suffering, and anxiety.

Men and women do not *fear* pain, suffering, anxiety or deep intimacy.

Men and women strive for deep intimacy with self, others, and meanings. They strive to learn how to secure love *in spite of* pain, fear, suffering, anxiety, and personal risk—they learn how to guide power and meaning toward and into the 'making' of love.

+ Making love for males and aging males is largely confined to sexual intercourse.

+ Aging males don't often deeply question what they don't do because they've adapted to what they already do and/or to laziness they can afford.

Vision of self for the young male:

Young males are ignorant.

Young males are ignorant of their ignorance and their underdeveloped courage.

Young males often use force and will to feel strong and independent.

They rightly seek ways to actualize themselves. They imitate what they long for: an identity, enhanced individuality, self-value, personal power, and developmental security as personal meaningfulness and belongingness.

They rightly admire aspects of toughness and bravery, and they tend to gravitate toward activities where physical strength, stamina, and determination are related to competing and winning. This is normal up to a point in the maturational process. But when time says 'embrace the new', young and aging males who haven't been appropriately taught and trained won't fully hear the call. They won't know how to 'see' reality's demand to give up aspects of the 'old' and connect dots for the new. They don't really understand that dots have to be connected *more and more* for living to get better and better.

Young males who do not meet a man-teacher *in any way* will become aging males who tend to emphasize clothing, possessions, behavior, attitude, and distorted versions of living and, therefore, loving.

But

If young males *seek* appropriate education and training, they'll discover their deficiencies and find a way to begin developing better vision for self. The problem is there are very few men. So what can a young male do?

Read. Study. Pursue. Don't quit. Keep going, no matter what. No mercy, no excuses. Do an MRI on your thinking and take action on the lab report you can't challenge.

On a personal note:

✦ My dad died when he was 52. I was there. Emphysema. He looked like naked poultry I'd seen hanging from hooks in European meat shops. Couldn't breathe or speak. Just stare and mouth words to me.

✦ Many years later, I said goodbye to my mom on a Wyoming December night while she was in the hospital. I knew I'd never see her again. I waved, turned, and left. Got in my diesel truck at 9 p.m. and headed for LA through a snowstorm. Two weeks later, she died.

✦ The next year, my brother went into the hospital on a Sunday and died on Tuesday from sepsis.

✦ The following year while driving my Dodge truck, I was informed about prostate cancer. I pulled over and at that moment decided to have it all cut out. And I did. Lost my medical virginity two weeks later, on a Thursday; came home on Saturday. Went to the gym on Tuesday. Refused painkillers.

✦ A year later, I had a hip replacement. Went in on a Thursday, home on Saturday, no painkillers. I was awake during the surgery. I walked the next day then did stairs. Took a walker to

85

the gym the following Tuesday. Not bragging. Just doing it.

✦ A year later, I moved back to Wyoming and started this adventure. Left a career, friends, family, routines, and comforts. Coming here included caring for my sister, a smoker for 50 years, on oxygen, and deep in stubbornness. She collapsed into a grisly decline that lasted two years. She went to hospice....there for almost six months. MRSA had colonized in her lungs. I had to wear a mask and gloves. Did all I could all the time. Watched her take her last breath and enter the inexplicable stillness of end.

What's the point of all this?

The point is, dying. No one's exempt.

The point is, living, living with fewer regrets.

The point is, we all go. And the point of that is: do we get the point of that point? Gone is gone. So cherish living. Learn to forgive. And give all your flowers to those you love before they hit the ground.

The point of living?

What is the point of living?

The point of living is living. Living now. The point of the now is to love. The point of that is: we carry now and we carry love. And if we make love for deep real that makes us deep real. If we don't make it, we lose it. When we lose love, we learn about living as a shade of gray where pain and darkness mingle. That feeling is death's silent message. It's short, to the point, and often so tragic: going to gone.

The message of gone is pervasive. We see it and hear it daily. Sometimes, we see our own going to gone in the mirror; we see the changes, our fade toward ending, toward wind.

I *get* the point of living. When I was younger, I sensed it but now I do get it, yes I do. And it's that point that partly drives me to write this book and do what I do.

So, as you have discovered or will discover, the point of living will connect you to your vision of self and, therefore, to the brokenness, mistakenness, or fullness of your....

Vision of Spirit:

Being human in today's world is more complicated partly because the word spirit and what it deeply signifies has been stiffened, rejected, trafficked, pimped, renamed, distorted, loosened, defended, or placed in foster care with dwindling numbers of persons able to see and guard its original scope and depth.

That said, please consider that the essence of 'spirit' *lived* is drive of courage caused by inside holiness aroused as reverence for goodness done naturally against the negative in you, others, the environment, and beyond.

The development of courage is demanding because love always puts you on the ground to sustain it here and now. To do that all the time takes raw strength and deep will casually referred to as determination.

If you do not, cannot, or will not risk fully for love, you can only speculate about love, long for it, grow for it, or quit and go bland.

If children lose the opportunity to learn how to think and how to love because of how they are taught and trained, the child loses. Then we all lose. That's the tragedy of human history. And preventing greater losses of love is the greatest challenge in today's increasing mire of negligence, hiding, disregard, dismissal, anguish, suffering, silliness, and malice.

Without the drive to love fully, love withers into degrees of loveless charity, loveless fucking, insecurity, anxiety, duty, obligation, sentimentality, and easy faith that can become an emotional pose, an intellectual premise, a fashionable straitjacket, a cozy way to belong, an identity tradition, a hiding place, a tool for a hustle, or semantic fruitcake no one wants to eat.

So....

Without the drive to love fully there can be no beautiful battle cry, only crying out. The outcries.

Most males don't understand a beautiful battle cry. But when any male sees a *man in action* in any way, he will envy, admire, and feel embarrassed or intimidated because the drive to love fully will be revealed as diminished or absent.

So think about

Going gauntlet, hardcore. That means learning how to choose to change all of your destructive thinking, habits, and actions....

Because

Without doing that, gauntlet will win. And you'll lose because of what you don't/won't change. If losing what *doesn't have to be lost* is okay with you, then throw in the towel now and coast till you die.

But if you are willing, then do it, knowing you'll stumble often and get hit hard. Keep rollin', always rollin' for the good, not your version of the good but the truest good. It takes time to learn what that means and it'll take all you've *got* but the sacrifice is worth the reward. Just get out of the way with all excuses and resistance, and begin.

Gauntlet facts:

All humans are faced with gauntlet. It's called being alive. If you aren't increasingly able to withstand and stand within the pressures of struggle, aiming, and achieving, gauntlet will win. It wins the minds and spirits of the rich, the famous, the influential, and leaders. We see that all the time. It's called the news.

When gauntlet says 'show up', most folks find a way to run and hide in work, fantasy, retreat, reputation, distractions, excess, career, ideology, busy-ness, competition, arbitrary thinking, weakened religion, criticism, anger, trivia, and a whatever.

If you don't do gauntlet hardcore, what's left? Money? Things? Sex?

And, eventually, what's left of you?

Suggestion for going gauntlet:

Stand tall, position yourself, look ahead, smile the deep smile of 'bring it on', and 'vision' your journey to its conclusion as the fullest manifestations of all the truly good you can do with your talent, passion, and choices. Do it hard. Make it happen.

Then, decades later, turn and look back at what could've taken you out—but *didn't*. What could have taken you out is you. That didn't happen because of your bravery and drive to love fully: 'staying in', holding on, and remaining.

This means that spiritual vision excludes:

Negatively destructive actions derived from negatively selfish thinking.

Negatively destructive actions caused by willful ignorance, rigid crudeness, ridiculous convictions, and abuse justified with defensive rationales and behaviors centered on force, aloofness, lies, physical or emotional violence, and/or the arrogant need/compulsion to win….all in the name of a self-styled, self-interpreted, self-proclaimed tiny-vision protected pathetically by the 'If you don't like it, fuck you and get out of my face' statement that can be said and done in many ways.

Moving right along facts:

Excessive personal gain *is not a relative topic.* Excess is not personally determined.

It's obvious.

Men *share* excess willingly, easily, and wisely with others, always from the heart.

Males calculate how to share. They downplay, deny, or dismiss being stingy or cheap.

Intentional ignorance is arrogance driven by fear and sustained by negative stubbornness, abuse, and force interpreted as valid power. Intentionally ignorant males rarely ask 'What's wrong with me?' then listen openly. They prefer to ask 'What's your problem?'

Unintentional ignorance is honest; it's the state of readiness for expansive education and training. That's what's so beautiful about children and youths: they want it.

We really are on our own for all the valid love we can make; and wherever that takes us and we take it, that's the journey, the adventure, and the education of our individuality, uniqueness, and greatness—a vision of the spiritual.

It takes about forty years to sense the road you're truly on. If you can't sense that by then, you're not on any real road yet; you're a version of stillness in motion on a maybe or you're just raw lazy and having conversations about whatever without saying anything real except words.

Negative stubbornness is negative *withholding*: keeping what could and should be shared, given, or done.

Positive stubbornness reinforces the continuity of integrity, dignity, and the truly good.

Negatively stubborn folks tend to be passive or active controllers who don't understand valid power as a 'container' symbolized by 'heart': that which contains you as you contain it. They don't understand that what fills a heart will, sooner or later, reveal that heart: more love, less love.

One aspect of personal and cultural tragedy is the vision-deformity that turns holiness into folks walking away from it.

Goodness is the least abstract of all abstractions because it is essentially who we are, what we do, and what we live for until we get messed up and lose integrity.

Most visions of reality, self, and spirit today need eye surgery, cranial liposuction, time for solitude and wild nature, and more viewing of the deeply worthwhile.

We all know living could be better, we all know how we'd like it to be better, and we all know why it doesn't happen more fully for....

ALL THE CHILDREN

Child

Something there is in a young child's eyes
Upon which our love completely relies.
Odd it is that we who know so much
Are by young eyes subdued, that we might touch
Love's truth and hold it. How like sacred light
Do young eyes upon us stare—we whose sight
So traveled, weary, and of restless rue
Made that we our global sadness renew.

In child, yes, we see heaven's pure return....
To old candles patient who gently burn
For time, before all longing into night
Is taken....I wish I may wish I might:

> Wee one I ask, please, into my heart teach
> How I for you can all my age impeach.

Consider:

If you're a parent of a young child, can you honestly say….'In your own way I want you to be just like me because I'm the example of everything you will want to become. I study and train to be the best person I can be. I defend truth only, not my version of it. I do this for myself and with others. I do it with you and for you. I do it because I love you. I know living isn't easy and aging won't be easy. I also know the meaning of living is in the history of how you live and love, and in the kindnesses you do along the way. So I say to you, my child, I want you to be completely like me in every way, but do it all *your* way. I give love, time, knowledge and training, and my protection to every aspect of who you are. I put you on my shoulders every day so you can see more of the world than I was able to see….because living is the adventure of receiving the gift of life and opening it into who you already are: a flower and a butterfly angel perched on a Rainbow I try to make for you every day.'

I wrote another poem:

When a child smiles, ready to leave,
It makes of a parent an old shirtsleeve….
A mingling of measures, photos, and clock….
A moment of smiles, tears, and lopsided talk….

The many years so short, so swift
Have come to this, and this small gift—
My song for you, little one, is done.
Listen closely to its loving refrain
As a prayer for you against all pain:
> 'Be safe, my child. Be well and strong.
> Live and love fully. Love deeply and long.'

Tomorrows will come again and again,
And I among them will go.
But you will live and hold from death
This song: its life has shaped my breath.
Learn it you will, and from joy you will cry
These same lyrics in a time of goodbye;
You'll stand alone, and sing the refrain
As I do now against all pain:
> 'Be safe, my child. Be well and strong.
> Live and love fully. Love deeply and long.'

A perspective:

Negligent parents harm children. If children recover, their struggle is harder....or they give up in particular ways without knowing what's being lost.

The highest regard neglected children can have for deficient parents is realistic disappointment that combines understanding, forgiveness, pity, and compassion into mature forms of goodbye to what could have been but never will be.

Facts:

If you remain unmarried to life, you are barren.

If you marry life, you will discover how to live in readiness for love.

That discovery will eventually introduce you to your 'children'.

You will love your form of 'children'.

You will produce goodness.

A thought about daily heroism:

Heroism is consistency in all things good every day, and that adds up to another day of dealing with everything and making good memories.

Men know:

Less love, more conflict;

More conflict, less happiness;

Less happiness, more suffering;

More suffering, less health;

Less health, more disintegration;

More disintegration, less fulfillment;

Less fulfillment, less good;

Less good, more evil;

And on and on....

Men know reality's only demand is to be realistic. To be realistic requires actions for the best mental health, the best physical health, the best pleasures, the best studying, the best exercise, and the best ways to preserve and enhance the best love.

On a personal note:

I was easily fascinated when I was a boy so I stared a lot.

The years passed and I grew taller in the presence of brutally destructive parents.

I became a young male scavenging for bits of truth-food.

Truth was around me and in me but I couldn't connect the dots because I was too young. I just 'sensed' it was there, somewhere. All I could do was the day-to-day because that's what kids do. And since I was fascinated by the immediate and the obvious, the day-to-day wasn't so bad despite my parents' behavior, language, and violence. And, somehow, I sensed a 'personal fact' I never dismissed because it felt like a promise that would be kept if *I* kept it—the promise was *me*. So I kept it.

At eighteen, I left the house and stayed away. Went to college, still loyal and still trying to help. But I really wanted to *go*—see the world and learn.

I started reading more, looking into, thinking about, listening closely-closer, watching everything, and hitchhiking physically and mentally to discover, discover, discover. It all felt natural to do, real. Yes, I was seeking, but I had no 'idea' what I was looking for within the thousands of hours that became so many books read, so much great music heard, so many museums seen, and so much aloneness lived. It was all part of a journey that felt like a big check I couldn't cash. But I kept going, enthusiastic, tired sometimes, and often feeling lost and an outsider.

I stood on many personal and real cliffs, cried from ignorance, pain, longing, and joy....looked at sunrises and sunsets in many countries, and kept on truckin' and searching, forever searching, seeking and studying.

Not once have I ever doubted the truth of beauty and the beauty of truth. I just didn't know how to say that when I was young.

That beauty/truth correlation began in me as my Wyoming. It's a metaphor, a symbol, a reality, and a way of functioning. And it's tattooed on my right forearm. Lucky is on my left forearm. The birth years and symbols for each daughter are tattooed on my left and right shoulders.

I live in Wyoming.

My granddaughter calls it Wyhoming. She's correct.

So once again, what do I *really know?*

Well, I know the biggest risk is learning how to love and how to love the struggle to love more until love starts to grow you into a gift you long to give.

And I know pain, like doubt, is a companion and an arrow pointing inward and upward as a reminder to arch toward the sun, always.

I know I'm seeking more peace, comfort, delights, and fewer bullrides.

I know when I'm challenged or can't sleep well, when anxiety crowds me, or I have to pause because of the possibility of dying before my work and love are done, I position myself and *ride* a living prayer out of the chute. I hold on, yes I do....I hold.

Sometimes the sound of the buzzer has taken years.

I've been thrown many times.

I know thud.

And I know a mature recipe....

Learn how to think.

Train.

Season time with abundant work, play, laughter, dance and song, friends, food, family unity, and joy.

Add reliable traditions and personal spice.

Mix well.

Serve warm.

Enjoy gratefully.
Repeat often.

I know....

Every day requires self-talk to stay centered and hold it all together no matter what's going on. This means everything has to be taken in and dealt with. It takes all you've got and asks for more. And you have to deliver. Or not. It's a choice. If you do it consistently, you'll be learning to:

Embrace inconvenience.
Be consistent in all things good.
Develop potency for the good.
Do what heals.
Seek the structures of truths.

I know kids need to know....

Morality isn't neurotic bondage to rules that imprison enthusiasm and vitality.

Morality is not self-destructive or self-sacrificing submission *in the name of love*.

Morality isn't a squeaky-clean lifestyle that reflects fearful adherence to 'laws', as though one is an endless child under endless scrutiny for disobedience, willfulness, and inappropriate questioning, dreaming, and delights.

Morality is not excessively dutiful, sentimentally absurd self-surrender to false authority and crummy parents.

Reality tries to tell us that we are not love's clay to be shaped according to misinterpretations of facts, self, others, the universe, and Truth.

Love, if understood accurately and lived appropriately, includes morality as wisdom *at war* with whatever threatens to negate the truly good and children.

Again, what *is* morality?

As stated, it's the centrality of goodness sustained flexibly and openly all the time.

Morality is truth's mail carried in the heart. And it waits within every sane person for arousal and expression in activities that are deeply worthwhile.

Morality is not relative, even though humans make it so.

Morality begins within the spontaneous urge to be authentically kind. If you don't want to give or be kind, don't. But figure out why.

Please know:

All deep and long-lived heroes give effortlessly and continuously. And they, like all great persons, make love transparent, luminous somehow, and for a moment the greatness of living feels really *intimate* as the poetry of reality: prayer without language and devotion without display.

All men study this poetry to learn how to rhyme with it.

Thoughts for reflection....

We all know that contemporary morality, like the word God, is imprisoned by the human mind. This, in turn, imprisons mind by making mind only about mind. Mind has become an overburdened word. It carries too much weight.

Freedom and love can be separated. When this occurs it's called negative time: the good and its potential are reduced, lost, or destroyed.

Negative time is present personally, nationally, and globally as the mismanagement of responsibility. We witness it every day on the news. We see it more locally in the ways folks talk and do. We see it in friends, family, and self. But we don't talk about negative time often, particularly to the mirror.

Whatever destroys the good is evil. Sometimes that action is real subtle and not even noticed, particularly in conversation and thinking.

Either you live primarily in and for true goodness or you live in self-styled versions of goodness but you include enough true goodness to avoid too much guilt, hypocrisy, shame, lying, and cops.

You are what you do. What you do reveals how you think. How you think reveals what you revere. That reverence further reveals that you're either going toward divine or demise, or you're compromised somewhere in between, and stressed.

Right now you might want to say....

'What's the point of all this? Who gives a damn about reverence and divine or demise? What the hell difference does it make? We're all just gonna die anyway and be forgotten like all the millions before us. We're like fallen leaves. Our anonymity is already complete. Our names mean nothing. So what's the point of all the questions? And who really cares about being a complete man? If it's so hard to do and sustain, why try? I'd sooner just have a lazier life, some good times, eat what I like, do what I want to do, and take what comes when it happens. And if I never become a complete man....oh well. So what is the *point*?'

The point is, *you will lose*. You are naïve.

If that's okay with you, and you're ready for what all that really means, rock on....

Men know that losing potential is not okay for young males.

Young males do *not* know that it's *not* okay to lose potential.

Men know that their most deeply personal obligation is to lift and hold the young higher for an introduction to the sacred world of dots. And they know that if you become who you truly are, you'll eliminate all silly questions and you'll be ready to lose your name, and it won't feel like a loss.

So, yes again:

The destiny of every child *is* to pass through gender to *stature*: from male/female to man/woman. That passage means:

Maturing is a struggle.

Living is a struggle.

So struggle for greater creative liberty to express your most deeply valid *passion*.

Then....

Learn to risk for truth, holiness, and children.

Flipside:

Resisting the opportunity to struggle is resistance to learning how to think, how to love, and how to embrace dependency as the strength for interdependency.

Therefore:

Struggle.

It's the only way to harvest what you have the privilege to plant: you.

A risk:

One essential aspect of struggle is the risk of learning to listen deeply—attentively, politely, and empathically, regardless of the circumstance or information; learn to listen beyond your reactions; listen to the speaker's words and *tone* so you can understand *why* and how the words are being said, and said to *you*. Listen to learn how to interpret the 'moment' accurately. Then you'll be more able to respond appropriately.

But....

If you're not really available for that risk, you'll experience distancing, frustration, annoyance, anger, impulse, confusion, impatience, and the urge to leave a conversation, circumstance, situation, or person. You'll leave when you should stay or you'll stay when you should leave. You'll talk when you should listen or remain quiet when you should talk.

Or you'll engage to win when you should surrender.

Or you'll be antagonistic, condescending, feisty, patronizing, abusive, sarcastic, forceful, and immaturely unrelenting when you should be humble and empathic, compassionate and willing.

Or you'll listen without listening, in a polite 'whatever' mode with head nods and mmhmms and yeahs. But you won't really care.

The deeper point is, if you do not remain *centered* and *engaged* all the time, you'll mismanage the chance to contribute to the making of the good. That means more difficulty.

Most folks don't really care about that little fact.

A few struggle-suggestions:

Dump vanity. I think George Bernard Shaw defined vanity as the fear of being left out or rejected.

State your sickness. Then do what it takes to heal.

Work your ass off.

Eat right, live right, stay healthy, and master self-discipline and the shovel so you can dig your way to Point B every day. In the best sense, that means do what you love as much as you can, love what you do, and do it all with someone you love in a setting you both love. Make some kind of great 'family', home, and community.

Learn how not to be offended or inappropriately dependent.

Change distorted viewpoints and behaviors.

Show up for every positive aspect of living.

Labor for love through learning to love the labor.

Use money wisely in all ways for the joys, reality, and opportunities it represents: options and generosity.

Discover what your shelters are. Dump false shelters.

Challenge your beliefs, loyalties, opinions, and convictions.

Decide whether you pimp anything, including yourself *in any way*....

    &

Analyze what dazzles you

    &

What thrills you.

If you struggle do all this, you'll discover that your skills and stamina are sufficient or deficient....

Love is what love does.

Love does what love is.

Love never destroys. Humans destroy.

Love never hurts; it only hurts when it's lost.

So, as the old saying goes, love like you've never been hurt.

What *is* forgiving...forgiveness?

What is it?

Genuine forgiveness is a verbal/spiritual action intended to reduce feelings of anger/regret/pain/

sadness/guilt/shame caused by the realities of an *injustice*. You can ask for it, you can give it.

A *valid* apology is an honest acknowledgement of the destruction of respect, trust, and love's potential because of language, action, and behavior.

A *deep* apology is making the effort to be received because of the pure, living *drive* to heal love's wounds and reintegrate with the *life* and *spirit* of the receiver—if it's not too late.

Initially, I forgive you means: 'I'm in motion toward forgiving you and it'll take time.'

Eventually, I forgive you means: 'I will forgive you, with or without you in my life. I'll make my decisions based only on that which is best, not what I *feel* is best. I will learn how to think better and not be a fool for love in any way.'

If successfully completed, forgiveness restores balance and heals relationship. Healing occurs only if forgiveness is purely offered and purely received. Most folks don't include that purity when they hear or say 'I'm sorry' or 'I forgive you.'

Deeper forgiveness permits past events to have *place,* duration, and value.

Deeper forgiveness helps organize time as past *place,* current *place,* and future *place* so a person can grow toward 'desired place'.

Deeper forgiveness entails the reduction, end, or renewal of *engagement* with a person for whom trust and respect are not or may not be adequately possible or desirable. What's left is pity: *compassion* united with acceptance of the true facts. No blur. If you do not create a reunion, you place that person's reality in your *history* as a resource and *move on* without condescension or animosity.

Move on means *grow* beyond the event, person, and yourself.

Sometimes, trust and respect are restorable, but when 'original' has been broken into broken, it's broken.

If that's the case, you....

Move on.

Change how you think.

Learn that the other person's problem is not *your* problem.

Learn that your problem is you.

Learn to work on you until there is no baggage, no animosity, and no vindictiveness.

Be clear. Be firm. Be honest.

Do all this until it's a way of living.

Keep it that way.

Celebrate your healing by renewing it every day.

On that note, consider:

'Original' is a paradise.

When a paradise is broken it becomes a paradise lost but remembered. Broken can be mended but 'original' cannot be *fully* restored. Mending original is difficult. It requires the desire to heal and forgive.

The *desire to heal* is the essence-drive in the battle cry for preserving the paradise of the wild beauty we casually call love.

Striving *for* love is what we call soul. Soul isn't a thing. It's more like a verb producing sun—trust for joy.

Trust protects every aspect of human paradise and it's the heartbeat of love in all relationships: self-trust, other-trust, reality-trust, Spiritual-trust. Children exemplify trust and joy *naturally,* spontaneously, and fully until that beautiful integrity is altered by what is casually called an adult.

Related to that:

My father, at a distance of eight feet, played Russian roulette with me when I was fourteen.

He carefully spaced the shells in four of six chambers, spun the chambers, flicked them closed, looked at me, slowly pointed the .38 pistol at my face, pulled the hammer back, paused, and squeezed the trigger.

Click.

He said, 'You were lucky that time, kid.'

Then he took another drink and chased it with Coke.

I am lucky.

Lucky a thousand times, but 'click' changed me, changed my 'original' to....what?

Part of paradise in me was broken.

Have I forgiven him? Yes.

Do I love him? No. I love what could have been.

Was I a loyal son? Yes. I tried only the way kids know—all out, almost blind with devotion and longing.

I've learned to leave each event in-its-place and keep each place in place when current reality stimulates tough memories, insecurities, fears, trust issues, and yearnings. Good memories can visit anytime.

So....

Yes, forgiveness *is* a tall call and the labors of love are a tall call. But love is all that matters because it's what all matter serves....and it must be protected for spirit to flourish because spirit can be broken. A broken spirit ends the person, animal, or environment.

Protecting spirit means learning how to let love *dance and sing you*—learning to follow love so love can lead, and leading with love so love can follow because the music and lyrics of heaven and earth are all we truly and most deeply 'have'. They are what we are until we start rewriting the lyrics, changing the notes and tunes, and re-choreographing the divine. To avoid doing that means asking all the basic questions, getting the answers, then putting them into the best actions—singing about heaven and earth through what you *do*. Otherwise, you never sing and dance in the deep real. That's what makes humankind so tragic....the great dancing and singing that could have been, then and now.

My father lived on both ends of a teeter-totter that tottered and teetered between sanity and the living presence of pure evil done with a malevolent smile and brutal actions.

My mother did what she did.

Both had goodness but it wasn't strong enough.

They unintentionally destroyed trust in every area of living.

Somehow I knew that the whole world wasn't as sick as my parents. I could see that. It was obvious. And I knew I wasn't sick like my parents. A bullet could take my life but physical, verbal abuse, and what my mother did couldn't take my eyes or spirit. There was no one to talk to about any of what went on, and nowhere to turn for comfort, but there was nature—Wyoming. I took it, took it all in.

In our house, God was a rumor I chose because it chose me and I said *yes*. So I'm still dancing and singing. This book is part of that motion.

Yes....

My parents gave what they had to give. And they have 'place' in me. I don't disturb that place. I let it be what it was so my 'is'—the now—is as pure as I'm able to make it.

I gave love to my parents but I couldn't love them. I longed for them then but I don't miss them.

He was an aging male. She was an aging female.

They never matured; didn't want it badly enough. I feel sadness for them. They lost out. Couldn't open up, change, see the light, grab it, and run with it the whole length of gauntlet. They quit and went into the dark, wounded and bleeding. They died there.

Surprisingly, from how I grew up:

I really wanted to be a father and make a home. But I was ignorant and unfamiliar with what all that meant. I had the love but not the info....so I winged it, did the best yessing I could—I went gauntlet. Still going gauntlet. So I love trying to write this book and the other books, I love teaching, my black '04 Dodge diesel, my Akita, my grandchildren, my daughters, Shea and Sadie, a few dear friends, this old cabin, the drama of nature wrapped in the rolling rhythms of tranquil and wild Wyoming weather, really good organic food shared, working out hard, and learning. It's all about yes.

As a kid....I remember evidence of yes everywhere but not attaching to any of it—the flowers, trees, sky, land, seasons, and wind that rolled across Wyoming and into my heart with such clarity that something in me was born. I didn't *attach* to any of it but metaphorically I *became* all of it and remain that way—hooked in to the soil of living like Shorty, a stray tree I planted last summer...hooked into the immediate as the now of loving, dreaming, and growing. That kind of rootedness made **me**....and **made** me want to see, hear, touch, taste, and *do* the whole world. My imagination had no censor and my curiosity had no adversary. I was a solo kid in the living prayer of fascination that made me want to *see* and *do-it-all*.

So, in my little kid yes-world, I started hitchhiking through Cody's small, sandstone library, corner of 11th and Sheridan. The vision and excitement born from those shelves took me halfway around the world....for three years, '65 to '68—in England, Ireland, Europe and Africa; on boats, trains, cars, long walks, and in buses. I was joyfully driven to *see*....and see it I did, saw it all on a hitchhike and a sparrow's budget. It was glorious. I was sad at times but I never felt sorry for myself because I'd never felt sorry for myself ever. There was always too much to see and learn, and I figured learning would always be harder for me….so I stayed with it. And experienced a lot of beauty and thud.

But….to go back for a minute to….

April, '65:

I'd been drafted for Vietnam (real good story here), reclassified by the Selective Service due to injuries, and told to stay in touch regularly….graduated in August from the U. of Minnesota, and on September 8th I left America on an older Italian ship—the Castel Felice—with a hundred bucks in my pocket, no way home….on a gamble I'd be accepted for study at a school in London.

I auditioned five days before school started. One spot open….auditioned in the morning….waited in the foyer till late afternoon….watched the others come and go. Then me, the last one….I went in and before the director and two teachers could say anything I passionately announced 'I don't want to chitchat or do courtesy. I got a lot riding on this audition so please just say yes or no.' The director said with a broad smile, hands raised, 'Yes!'

I ran out, down the street, ran back and apologized for not thanking them, then spent half my money and took the overnight train to Paris….at around

7 a.m. I rolled into Gare St. Lazare, got off the train and noticed 'They all speak French'. I laughed and thought, that's because I'm in France! Wow! I was amazed. Europe was real. Walked all day, ate little. Marveled....returned to London.

Three years of study began.

The story attached to that dream coming true includes Sir Tyrone Guthrie and two other deeply generous persons whom I thank even though they've all passed. What happened was, like the draft incident, another 'miracle'. About that—I stayed in touch with the Selective Service. I was not a draft dodger. I didn't and don't dodge anything requiring attention.

In 1967, after almost two years away, I nervously re-entered America because my father was dying. A month after I arrived he died.

I hitchhiked to Victorville, California....stayed with a friend for a weekend, hitched a ride back to LA with hippies in a VW bus all painted out, got arrested on 7th and Grand in downtown LA.... and went to old LA County Jail....as a felony suspect, robbery...did a full on, classic interrogation in a tiny room without windows, only a naked light bulb hanging from a cord above me and a bulky, aggressive detective....went to trial....the charge was reduced to a misdemeanor....no checking on my draft status (there's more to this story)....I got out, hitchhiked to New York, and returned to Europe via Shannon, Dublin, the wild Irish Sea at storm-time, and Wales....then London. Exhausted. One year to go, no desire to quit.

Kept on studying....traveling the yesses, foraging, in and out of homelessness, but always with deep *enthusiasm* for seeing....and it took me all the way into numerous epiphanies so timely in their inducements of 'existential grandeur' that the hardships were worth it. I was really okay.

Then it happened, that one wonderful I-am-*alive* moment, on the end of an isolated, deeply southern, really old and remote Italian pier at sunset. There I stood, staring at the motionless Mediterranean Sea and distant horizon....as though both were the door to something I was seeking, and telling me I carried the key. I stared at waning sunlight....received the moment, felt the lock open and open me....and there I stood, mute and in awe.

I said, 'I exist. I exist....people.'

I cried.

And started hitchhiking north.

That half hour in southern Italy was the beginning, the truest spiritual beginning of the last fifty years. It was a turning point that has played its part in why

I'm in this chair in front of this computer in this log cabin where windows reveal the beige-gray prairie silence of late Autumn.

A second but slower turning point was due to the lady on 50th St.

So....

Did I have 'anger issues' when I was younger? You bet. I didn't know how to love fully or openly, or how to join the norms. But I tried. Tried hard.

I carry deep *regret* for my mistakes. I know sorrow.

On that note, here we go:

When I was about to become a father I made a vow not to let the 'devil' of my parents pass through me into my children.

Then, fifteen years later, BAM! *The* most difficult action of *all my years* occurred when I told my daughters I would be leaving our home and getting an apartment. Never have I known such pain.

In their eyes was the holiness of all children.

I was reducing that holiness in *my* children. I was reducing their trust of *me*.

I could *see* that. There was no way to deny the reality of my younger daughter's eyes revealing the process of a breaking heart.

I knew I had to become steel to withstand the pressure of their pain that revived my childhood pain. I became a no-rust, no-bend commitment to heal their brokenness until the day I die. I was not guilt-driven; I was love-driven for them. Still am.

I began to walk the walk more, walk all the extra miles to make wrong as right as right could be—only for them, for their *eyes* that had told me what I'd said could not be undone, taken away, reduced, or changed....

I vowed to hold their spirits into the light of love as completely as I could....forever.

I was deeply willing and available.

I gave me to them. Gave. Kept nothing for myself and refused to criticize their mother.

I held them both, even when they were not with me.

I labored, driven by love and love's pain. I was *determined*.

I entered the question of self and the question of God whole hog, all out, 100 percent.

I felt guilt, shame, remorse, sorrow, ignorance, and the full burden of broken love...*again*.

They had trusted me. I had failed them. Broke some original in them.

I wish I could have read this book back then.

Unknowingly, I intensified my willingness to train myself to do only what was best, *no matter the effort, cost, or pain.* Every choice *mattered.* I was *in.*

I knew I needed to learn how to think better and love better. I didn't consciously say that to myself and I didn't know what to study or where to go for answers, but my drive was deep and unstoppable. It was a spiritual quest for the preservation and proliferation of love in my daughters' eyes and hearts and futures.

I had to *grow.* All I knew was yes.

The shock of everything was a new kind of love wilderness called the reality of what I'd set in motion because of my choices. And I had to take the hits, deal with it all, and never back down, away, or out of my vow.

It was *pure* struggle, day and night. And it was hard pain, the kind that tears the heart like we tear paper. More pain was the last thing I wanted. But my love for them and my desire to see their eyes restored to full light was indomitable, indefatigable. That meant I would not fail because I would not yield. Ever.

I was immature and ignorant when I had proposed marriage with a sandwich to their mother. I didn't know then how deeply *ignorant* I was; like an orphan confronted with what should be more familiar but isn't. The logic of the obvious had always surrounded me and I'd always struggled to honor it. All I had was a willing heart, a strong body, and blunt, unconquerable determination. Somehow, I'd preserved all three against the negative since childhood.

But the shock of seeing *more of the reality dots* because of divorce told me that things really needed connecting or so much would be lost unnecessarily and irretrievably.

And it was mostly all on me, all on the line.

So....

At forty-five I was in 'divorce gauntlet'. Had to start all over—personally, financially, and spiritually....not for me but for them. I wouldn't get to 'me' for twenty more years. I recognized I'd never really enjoyed 'getting to me'. And that was okay. But it wasn't okay. My whole focus was: they had to learn how to think better than I, learn how to love better than I, learn how to 'see' better than I.

I was in the dynamic of an amazing grace—struggle-stumbling from blindness to sight. Yes, I made mistakes but I never missed an opportunity, not *one* that I know of, to infuse my daughters' minds and spirits with the presence of education, training, perseverance, courage, and love. That concern has never waned. To this day, if they really need me, I'll jump in my truck and drive. They know that.

Two

If all treasures of this world's best were mine,
And treasures all I could after life know,
I would without pause keep only two.
Of equal worth they mirror all Design;
In union they transcend all wealth. Apart,
They're undiminished. Within holiness
They live in answer to God's only wish,
Which He has shared to me: it fills my heart
And marks my years, telling me what to do.
Perhaps from a star, I will see the two;
Them I will praise; not mine to give away,
Not mine to keep, only mine to say:

> Their touch is Nature; they are the Waters;
> Their seed is true; they are my daughters.

I have placed them in sunlight and tried to teach them how to cope with darkness. They're okay now. Good persons, good mommies, and becoming women. I've told them more than once and in differing ways:

Lead with love so love can follow; follow love so love can lead

And

Pain, suffering, struggle, and forgiveness will open love in you and help your blossom bloom if you handle it all in the right ways at the right times all the time

And

If pain, suffering, struggle, and forgiveness do not open your love, you'll begin to die unloved and unlovable

And

If your love is small and your words of love are big, you're on the way down, all the way to out and into the kind of aloneness money cannot alter

And

If anyone really looks into your eyes, they'll see who you are

And

No one can hide from eyes really looking to see. Look to see reality so you can remain you....centered. That's how you grow into your independence, beauty, strength, courage, and greater love: fully available for humans and for living.

So....

What have I learned? What do I know, *really know*?
Well, I know I've learned a lot.
And I know this book is more than halfway done.

Related to dot-connecting:

About eight years ago I was sleeping in a tiny trailer here in Wyoming. I had to take a leak. Opened the door, let loose, finished, then looked up and saw what is not believable logically: the clear night sky held the constellations, yes, but this time with a radical difference—all stars were connected by luminous lines. I looked away. Then I looked again. The lines remained. I nodded, stupefied....and accepted what I'd seen: the inexplicable interconnectedness of it all. It was a universal grid, and it included me. I didn't sleep that night; just listened to wind rock the tiny trailer back and forth....and remembered the Mediterranean Sea.

A perspective:

Independence is a short-changed word often confined to an idealized interpretation that hides serious insecurity behind pretend cool or some other form of aloofness dramatically on display.

Independence is the courageous recognition, acknowledgement, and integration of mortality: dealing with the big aloneness of being alone as one. Out of 'alone' comes the profound longing to be-long—to be *with-in* rather than with-out, and to become dependent and interdependent interpersonally, inter-spiritually, and wisely by doing what's worthwhile.

That means....

Live. Love. Heal.

Be willing to be deeply honest. Take action to stay that way. Otherwise....

You'll find ways to *hide*. You'll continue your routines. You'll be more troubled.

You'll be lonelier even though you might be in a relationship, had a wedding, became a parent, or are deeply committed to faith-service. You won't listen openly because you'll be in *discontent*.

Discontent is not a minor state like annoyance. It's serious. And it's a global epidemic in the male population. Has been for centuries.

Loving living means learning to relate loving to discovering the truly true, then repeating the living actions of loving for further discovery and deeper loving. That's how love-is-*made,* how it 'grows', and, therefore, how we grow and heal.

We all are, like all natures in this universe, meant to grow. If we do not grow we reverse love: we become our history.

Related to that:

We all know living is often more troublesome than it should be. Why? Well, because of misplaced emphases that cause one or more of the following negatively stressful states: unhappy, empty, lost, confused, depressed, pissed off too much, critical, sarcastic, violent, argumentative, confrontational, defensive, unjust, harsh, rejecting, unavailable, out of control, arrogant, greedy, negatively stubborn, negatively lazy, blameful, cynically critical, petty, needy, abusive, controlling, fearful of involvement and commitment, vain, self-sacrificial, narrow of mind and spirit; stingy, cheap, and knee-jerk fearful of that profoundly beautiful experience—hardcore *intimacy*. Hardcore intimacy is one-directional: in. Most folks never go all the way into intimacy: the wild beauty of self, love, and growth.

About that:

Men do not fear intimacy's risks.

Males tend to fear deep interpersonal intimacy. They prefer business, recreation, humor, entertainment, sports, and hobbies or collecting as sources of intimacy that aren't risky.

Females tend to tolerate male fear of intimacy and adapt to its limitations by accepting limited and limiting love.

Males fearful of deep intimacy tend to intensify self-control to reduce exposure to deep intimacy. The more a male is 'in control' the more out of control he actually is. This aspect of self-deception can easily cause him to believe he is strong. He wouldn't do well in wilderness. He'd be careless. He'd break down.

'Out-of-control' means the *need to control* is running the show, you can't stop it, don't know how to, don't want to, or, more sadly, you believe you're not out of control. And you want others to accept you *without resistance*.

If you're a controller and you meet a man and he really looks at you, you will quickly know he can see your disguise. You'll sense you cannot conquer him. You can only kill him. Maybe. So you hang in, dither, tolerate, try to get to know him, or you split.

Guaranteed—if you're an out-of-control type, you'll end up becoming a way of living you won't like.

Hardcore out-of-controllers walk tall on really short stilts. They like to strut. But, like all stilt-walkers, they fall because they don't understand or accept that they're on stilts. When they fall, sadly, no one really seems to care.

That said....

The weaponry for protecting meanings and intimacy is in the drive and actions of dignity and integrity. They are indomitable. They win all good battles, all good wars.

Meaning and intimacy centered in the truly good help to refine reasoning toward the beauty of the truly valuable: meanings sought, secured, lived, and defended.

If truly good meanings aren't received, understood, and implemented intimately, living begins to include aspects of the morbid.

Morbidity is a rough reality. And it's so commonplace that its presence as normalized madness is culturally and personally accepted in politics, religion, science, commerce, theology, psychology, education, entertainment, conventional worship, false art, budgets, families, relationships, beds, and solo.

When morbidity is present, less of living and loving are *cherished,* and reasoning becomes more arbitrary and/or more rigidly defended, out of which comes the personal lies that are fully true all day, every day.

We all know there are no lies and no one's a liar until the lie is revealed.

And we know:

The beat of human history goes on—

After profit, pleasure, and war, children get what's left—what they get is left out and left behind.

That's real morbid.

However, if you're fortunate, you learn that....

Intimacy can 'live' *us* the same way a song sings the singer so the singer can sing the song, and the musical instrument plays the musician, and the sport plays the athlete so the athlete can compete, and the part plays the actor so the actor can portray a person, and possibility thinks the thinker so thought occurs spontaneously and expressively.

Only the arrogant or naïve believe they sing the song, play the music, compete the sport, act the role, think the thought.

All authentic action is brought *forth* from the human. This is the 'drive' we casually call desire.

Desire-is-*beautiful* because it is the motivation-genesis of and for the possible. It is how we feel the worth of soul.

Implications:

As you know, if you don't live for what's possible and truly good, you go toward stale and resigned; you start to shrink.

All true lovers desire to express greater and greater meanings during aging because the process of increasingly mature play demands it.

Mature play is most sophisticated and complete when playing with a child. The holiness of encounters with children can cause happy crying. When that occurs, you see, with wordless clarity and profound appreciation, how reality and spirit, love and meaning, truth and beauty, and the infancy of power are in union with, from, and beyond the concept we call time. And it's all *in* the child you're playing with and watching.

Sometimes, when we're with children, we automatically reflect on the vitality we had when we had it all—when we were kids.

Children do not adequately learn:

If moral development is insufficient, persons are in self-conflict.

If moral development and struggle are separated, the result is havoc.

The separation of the words mind and spirit is culturally and personally accepted. The separation tacitly sanctions arrogance.

Arrogance is global. It always leads to defensiveness and the loss of love.

Arrogant persons develop sham-love.

Sham-love is in the falseness of wealth, in the falseness of conformist involvement, in the falseness of force regarded as power, and in fake commitments made to preserve stability, enhance personal gain, and secure approval.

Sham-love often includes self-proclaimed adherence to religion.

Sham produces folly. Folly is the domain of fool. Many fools are conventionally successful and influential, admired, neurotically adored, and followed. Or feared.

Resistance to the realities of *true* morality reveals the thinker as confused, arrogant, and/or rigidly opinionated—not 'open'.

True morality is rarely discussed seriously or deeply. The uptight and the self-righteous beat the topic to death in the name of goodness and never really ask the big-risk questions, starting with 'Could I be mistaken in any way about what and how I believe, and are my opinions really valid?' The lazy blow off the topic.

Resistance to conventional morality is based on resistance to interference, intrusion, and silliness. That's why conventional morality-talk is correctly regarded as an outdated nuisance to be avoided.

Again:

Morality defined: it is the experiential centrality of the truly good flexibly sustained.

Children need to learn:

Misinterpretations of morality diminish the dignity, integrity, and beauty of living.

Misinterpretations of morality and reality negatively reinforce fear and immaturity.

Misinterpretations of morality and reality are, by degrees, the voices of the deadly—persons who express anger and ignorance, unhappiness, resentment, belligerent stubbornness, rigid righteousness, the pimp-fictions of extreme conservatism or liberalism, and fear of the valid, realistic new. They prostitute language into combinations of words that appeal to ignorance, sentimentality, conformity, loyalty, obedience, safety, neediness, preference, habit, convenience, fear, resentment, anger, bias, frustration, abusive humor, increased cynicism, and/or the dismissal of an alternative viewpoint that is deeply realistic. Their voices curtail the potentiality of love. This is so wrong. And it means that....

The deadly, in varying degrees....

Are morally atrophied.

They have no deeply valid beloved *in any form*.

They are users, liars, and closed, cold, or dramatic hustlers.

They are the word-whores. If word-whores don't grow beyond their refined pimp-antic hustle, they accomplish empty, no matter how it's measured.

Word-whores are everywhere. So are the followers, the fools. Check it out.

With that in mind....

Think back on the meaning of *virtue*: supreme toughness used to preserve the good. For a man or a woman, it's this 'toughness' that disciplines mind/spirit and body to serve *the truly good*. Toughness inevitably includes actions of compromise and sacrifice—*valor*.

Valor through bravery shapes the battle cry of virtue.

Word-whores think they already know that and how to make the sound. They don't. They're not men.

Please know....

A lot of pretend men emphasize 'toughness' because that's all they've got to hold on to. So they make toughness prominent by verbal and/or physical force applied to subdue, intimidate, manipulate, and conquer. Many aging males *are* kick-ass tough but they don't take their toughness toward valor then into virtue. They remain stunted and defensively aggressive.

Any win for a pretend man is always a minor win, irrespective of fame, wealth, or position—unless he decides to become a more complete man. Then there's potential to shift from minor win to major win, from accomplishment to achievement, from tough toward valor to virtue, and from victory to triumph.

That sequence is more rare than rare.

When a man initiates the silent battle cry of virtue, it goes way beyond male 'tough' and 'cool'. It makes both words seem juvenile because it's not an act.

Disciplined drive to get beyond 'tough' produces more complete strength and reveals to willing males their potential for self-heroism—walking the walk into the gauntlet of manhood until they die.

Kick-ass tough related to the truly good always points to the male's potential for valid power—action related to the initiation, proliferation, and preservation of love.

Kick-ass tough that's not related to greater meanings is the sickness of a brute, big or little: rich, white collar, blue collar, no collar.

In other words....

Tough males are solid candidates for becoming strong men. But tough is not enough. And neither is strong.

Tough is a state of immaturity: durability, determination, and stamina related to small purpose.

Strong is related to courage based on embracing more meaningful purpose. Love.

When tough and strong unite in the quest for complete manhood, they are part of a greater purpose and greater meanings. That's where the real battles are initiated 100 percent.

If that percent is not in you, do what you can and put up with the results. But if you do decide to go for more complete manhood, do it every day until you die.

Then you will be *strong*: doing the words you live by.

And you will be *tough*: whatever comes your way you can deal with it and stay *centered* for the truly good.

You will be an example to yourself before you bring yourself fully and humbly to the lives of others folks, particularly the ones you-say-you-love.

So....

If you decide to become a more complete man, do *the basic actions*:

No violence or verbal or physical abuse *ever*.

No force, sarcasm, or arguing to reduce the pain of *your problems*.

No use of money to anesthetize the pain of your insecurities.

No manipulation of anyone for anything.

No distancing from any person you-say-you-love.

No lies, no deception, no excuses.

With those basic actions in mind, more aging male facts:

A man gives unbroken, definite proof of love to those he loves. His love is defined.

A male gives things and vague proof of love but not the full, pumping heart of *genuine* and *generous devotion*.

Most aging males don't understand how and why they're negatively or passively resistant to maturing fully, and why they're ready to argue about that or stay away from the topic by dismissing its importance in favor of narrow, personal, and self-protective bunker-agenda comments and shallow reasoning.

Aging males can be blandly serious, super good at talking sincerely, seriously defensive, passively aloof, very understanding and reassuring, and rigidly fixed in behavior, viewpoint, language, thought, and actions that reinforce the familiar and intensify its routines for personal security and stability.

Aging males are often vulnerable to the fact that they have only minor experiences of sufficient personal power and, therefore, of love. That's why aging males tend to be testy, more interested in money, defensive, passive, aloof, sentimental, combative, excessively competitive, private, resigned, critical, unable to forgive beyond an inch or two, and often need to have the last word, even silently, *or* they retreat from encounters that arouse any awareness of deficient personal power. Or, sadly, they say they don't care.

Aging males often try to find substitute replacements for deficient personal power by intensifying aspects of living that feel like personal power others can witness. They often need approval to perpetuate self-illusions and sustain fantasies of self-importance. They can be very needy. Or they've given up on what I'm writing about and settled for whatever they can enjoy with whatever money they have.

Aging males unable to secure external endorsement will retreat from most daily power encounters and find fantasy participation vicariously in the cool of *others* who embody specific male longings.

Or none of this will matter as long as the male can find enough simple pleasures to take the edge off of standing on the edge.

Aging males afflicted with temper need to learn: don't confuse being a man with your version of what you think a warrior is. Warriors are great, truly great spirits, not rinky-dink versions of a fighter. Tempers are not admirable. They're immature. And fights are just fights.

Battles are more significant.

Valid war is the summit.

That's where the men are because that's where the big meanings are. And valid war is always about deeply valid meanings—it is *virtuous war,* action to preserve the integrity and sanctity of life; it's the basic war we all encounter every day. Ultimately, it's the war for all the children.

The world has dodged that war.

That said....

Men embrace inconvenience.

Males tolerate inconvenience unless it's for personal gain financially or sexually.

Men live for and into the validity of valid power.

Men do not brag or long for approval and acceptance: they're not vain.

Men know the 'new' is inevitable so they're willing to change and adapt.

Men know the 'making' of goodness is not inevitable.

Men know the making of goodness is the creative beauty of freedom.

Men know when *love* is made the promise of love is kept.

Men know the promise of love is the only promise worth keeping because it keeps all other promises.

The promise of love is: if you seek it, *you will know it when it happens, and it will happen.* It will stop happening when you stop seeking. And you'll really feel it, feel the unhappiness, the discontent.

All this related to mastery and maturing....

Men know that remaining centered in self and goodness represents the complexity of the integrity and unity inherent in the mastery of being a man.

They know that remaining centered requires accurate perceptions, interpretations, and actions continuously balanced for rebalancing within the flow of all realities.

Men know mastery within one's humanity cannot be centered excessively on any one of the following: reasoning, spirit, habits, principles, beliefs, rituals, convictions, conventions, money, symbols, feelings, or aesthetics. Balances must be achieved and flexibly sustained because reality, like wild nature, is flux within sameness toward its new. And all flux for humans can only be resolved through the evolution of integrity and dignity: from matter all the way to mattering—the manifestations of all truly valid meanings lived.... then taught to children.

Men know that the senses, especially intuition, are essential for the unions of reasoning and vision.

Men know that taking appropriate action, including stillness and silence, preserves centeredness of self and enhances the possibilities for further goodness, happiness, fulfillment, mastery, and *joy*.

Men know that periods of solitude, reflection, meditation, and contemplation enhance all efforts, aims, pursuits, and communication.

The lie facts:

Most persons lie in very subtle ways.

Many chronic liars, as stated, build pimp careers on the manipulation of facts, ideas, principles, values, symbols, institutions, money, laws, and other humans.

The lie is the weapon of the lazy and the cowardly, irrespective of formal education, background, class, status, fame, and position.

The lie is unavoidable. From world leaders in all fields to all professions to all corporations to the streets and all homes, and to the 'throwaway' categories of persons in all nations, the lie is omnipresent.

Cultural stability depends on sustaining particular lies that arouse beliefs used to defend against facts that threaten cultural norms. That's how societies evolve, how leaders secure followers, and how politics works.

Challenging the lie begins with challenging the self-lie.

Challenging the self-lie is the mark of the will to mature.

Defeating any lie is a mark of progress.

In marriage there is no lie.
In wedlock there are lies.
Often, one of the lies is the declaration 'I love you'.

A man can spot a liar easily: it's in the eyes, *voice*, tensions, and arrogance present as mild or prominent indifference, defensiveness, or smooth.

A man can see the tensions and helplessness of a liar seeking engagement to be shaped and guided manipulatively for self-protection and self-advantage.

Many aging male liars and controller-cowards are in positions of great influence and authority, but rarely are they in the presence of a valid man. When that occurs, they know it, usually resist it, and dismiss the man even though they may act otherwise.

But they do not forget the man because the encounter with him reveals personal sham.

So....

What **is** a man?
What **is** a woman?

A perspective:

Education is maternal. The woman teaches.
Training is paternal. The man trains.

Teaching/learning and training/applying are interdependent activities that are understood accurately, respected fully, and *mutually shared* by a man and a woman.

Consider....

Maturing is the *only* positive 'path'. If you're not maturing, what's your path?

You are married to what dominates your time, thoughts, and actions. In the end, the meanings you have chosen to serve will serve as your mirror—they will reveal you for who you really have been. They're your self-portrait. So, if you get naked about what you've loved most and it doesn't love you back, it's because it can't. That's the lab report for mistaken emphases.

Aging males who overtly or covertly sacrifice children, females, and love are the crudest and most deadly of cowards.

Please know....

All children have the *right* to *play*. Play is the weaponry, wand, and aria of desire to be used for the magic of passionately singing the most personal song called self.

Many children partially lose that right because of the chronic ignorance and crudeness that permeates living with aging males/females who are careless or negligent parents.

If the 'right to play' is curbed, inappropriately limited, harshly judged and controlled, or taken from a child, that child will—and you can count on this—find a way to play. Or they will submit to the loss of play and become messed up.

If a child rightly and defiantly declares the right to play, the results will go one of three ways: creatively— they'll reach for the stars anyway; destructively—they'll slowly move toward darkness while looking back at disappearing light; or they'll become a yoyo, a motion-mix of dark and light, up and down, and circles.

Without play, the good in us never fully matures.
Without play and the good, we never fully mature.

How do men play?
Men play for keeps.
How do males play?
Males play to win.

Related to faith....

Faith is not an add-on, an acquisition, an external to be put in place, explained, used, and unrealistically imposed on children.

Faith is the deepest goal of education.

Greatest faith stands on the shoulders of all religions and all reasoning; then it climbs air, space, and beyond.

So....

The most realistic approach to faith is to get all the major-basic-majestic facts straight. Then get out of the way of how facts point to the truth that is *essential* and non-negotiable. Then line up more and more *realistically*. This means change your thinking *by questioning everything receptively*. This implies the effort to mature, and it's what 'seeking' most deeply means.

Consider:

Seeking is the basis of worship. It is the deep desire-drive toward and for the good, then into it. Once 'in', you find what is casually called truth. It'll drop you to your knees. And you'll learn to walk that way, protecting truth.

Seeking rhymes with doing, giving, and receiving: conquering self. You will have no faith-fort. You will live exposed, asking.

So....

Shallow is what shallow does.
Deep is what deep does.
Love is what love does.

Shallow presupposes depth.
Deep includes shallow.
Love absorbs both.

Related to desire....

Desire is the core of all faith. It is the creative drive of life in each of us. How we handle that drive is personally and culturally complex.

Desire is wings. We either fly then soar or we chain desire to a steel post and invent false flying.

Desire chained causes the false flights of the uptight, the judiciously litigious, the self-righteous, the naïve zealots, the shutdown ones, the tyrants, the deeply suspicious, the ultra-conservative, the condemnatory, the self-sacrificial ones, the overly willing, the punitive, the needy, the pleasers, the angry, the negatively rebellious, the discontent, and the crazy.

Full circle reiteration....

The destiny of the male is to become a man.

You're a young male, a pretend man, an aging male, or a man.

If you're not becoming a more complete man, you're in position to initiate that effort whenever you choose.

There are very few men in the world. All men are heroes.

To the extent you're not engaged in securing, preserving, protecting, and producing love, you're engaged in shades of folly.

Folly is the domain of fools. We're all fools at times.

When a male begins to learn how to appreciate and *preserve* the sanctity of pleasure, laughter, sexual love, friends, delight, play, intimacy, and *joy*, he's in position to begin to become more of a man and *protect* the sanctity of love by organizing living to serve that sanctity. This is outreach toward holiness....arms around the Sequoia Tree. Everyone's arms are long enough. Usually, it's the mind that's too short because it's tied up.

What *is* holiness?....

Holiness is when we *experience/see* into the 'how and why' of living on the ground but beyond the ground. Call it love. When holy happens, it teaches us so we can teach *all the children*. Then the holy becomes the sacred.

Facts:

False men are easy to spot.

False men wear mental and physical costumes.

False men tend to gravitate toward other false men who wear the same costumes.

If males are easy to spot, what are the male costumes/masks? Look around at other males, at their costumes/masks: physically, behavior, fashion, tatts, attitude, values, language, walk, status, possessions, symbols, humor, and the way they talk. You'll see what you need to see and hear if you're honestly looking and listening. Then call it like it is and go talk to a mirror about your costume/mask—your 'image'—and the why of it.

When false men make heroes of other false men, false manhood is reinforced.

The followers and imitators of false men do not seek reality. They tolerate it and work with it or go around it.

False men do not challenge their own lies.

Females enter wedlock often believing the males are or will be men, which means the question of actual manhood is never asked for real, never discussed until behavioral deficiencies, attitudes, and language cause the question to be prominent and pertinent.

Females wishing the males they wedlocked would become more complete men are females in discontent: potential women. They want completeness.

When an aging female meets a man, she either desires to become a woman through/to/for/with him, *or* her fear of becoming a woman keeps her female, *or* she doesn't even know how to define man or woman, so meeting a man goes over her head—she doesn't really get it, but she does get a lasting impression she can't explain. It's called attraction.

When an aging male meets a woman, he knows she is superior in strength and courage, and he either wants to avoid her, criticize her, destroy those qualities, have sex, and/or be taken care of by her.

So, in review:

This book challenges all lies and assumptions related to being a man. The challenge is intended for every male reader who has the humility and courage to question his manhood.

For young males, the alternative to manhood, as American culture reveals, is to become an imitation man or an aging boy. A guy.

For males who pose as men, this book is a direct challenge to take off the costume/mask and stand honestly naked as you *really are at this time in your life*. Then ask the right questions and take appropriate actions.

For aging and older males who are troubled, with or without money, this book is a call for re-training your mind/spirit to ask the right questions, *the basic ones*, listen to the answers, and begin the task of maturing.

So....

If you are willing to ask the basic questions and be truly honest with your answers, then willing to stand alone, then willing to struggle to think more accurately, then willing to take action—if you are *truly willing* instead of temporarily interested, then the topic of being a man is really important to you. And you will want to get...

MORE TO THE POINT

ASK AMERICAN MALES over thirty, what's a man?

The answer usually is predictably general and vaguely specific because the question unintentionally has been avoided, and everyone already 'knows' what a man is anyway, so why even ask?

The usual assumption is that manhood comes with aging, a beard, earning money, sexual potency, virility, durable reliability in relationship, and being sensitive, fun, humorous, and somehow 'tough' enough.

That's mostly true.

So what's missing?
And what's the big deal if....

The world's aging males call themselves men, nearly all females call the world's aging males men, teenagers and youths think older males are men, and overestimating the male is a dominant fact in all cultures.

The big deal is....

Pain, confusion, costly mistakes, loss of potential, and the destruction of others, mothers, and children.

If all that's not a big deal, what is?

And what's missing is....

The drive to keep it real, the drive to crack the nut, the drive to embrace the courage to change when change is required, the drive to serve integrity and dignity, and the drive to wage war for all the children.

More to the male point:

Driven males seek success in terms of abundance and acquisitions.

This is shallow.

Driven males protect shallow success and as though it has great meaning.

This is weak.

The protection of shallow success is always destructive.

This is immoral.

Stingy and cheap males know this but deny its *implications* because the facts indicate a shallow self-portrait.

All of this culminates in differing kinds of emptiness that lead to spiritual anorexia, a withering of being into chronic discontent and hiding.

The hiding places of the discontent are: habits, job, busy, lazy, denial, money, comfort, ignorance, self-inflation, anger, things, control, submission, fantasy, fear, force, influence, pose, and that great but nearly lost concept....idolatry.

Females can spot males in the presence of a man because the male will, one way or another, reveal his insecurity and immaturity.

Females truly seeking a man also seek womanhood.

Males seeking females very often seek maternal females who are durable and do not challenge male discontent.

Or they seek a female who can be controlled, one who understands and responds to expectations, rules, a leash, and/or, finger-snap, and will take abuse.

Or they seek temporary encounters without deep commitment.

Or they seek a fantasy.

Males and aging males to old males rarely discover lasting aspects of living that make them fully *bow*.... then lie prostrate in silence.

A man enters matrimony as an opportunity to take his *place* before a woman.

He knows his true height will then be on his knees.

So what is marriage
in contrast to matrimony?

Marriage is the evolution of deep willingness to be in full union for/with goodness.

Marriage represents the education of desire and the readiness to use reasoning fully for the proliferation of deep, valid love.

Marriage to a mate becomes the most interpersonal 'making' of love.

To make love means to be *made* again and again, and again into goodness: be 'made' toward more making. To do this, on the ground, is the labor of love for love.

To make love this way unites the three modes of time. In one sense, this is joy. Joy transcends time. It can't be endured for long. It absorbs one's being while releasing it. It's that powerful, that magical, and that mysterious. It's the deepest positive stress. It moves us within a *miracle* of awareness but beyond thinking. It holds us there for a *moment*, in union with truth we can only feebly articulate later as some aspect of holiness.

Joy heals.

Similarly, great art can, when we're ready for it, 'live' toward us as time, no time, motion, stillness, and power and meaning received concretely, abstractly, and spiritually. It enters us and really penetrates; we respond toward it and match it: we bring to it what *we* are. And that is the meaning of rhyme. It is the motion of union. We unite *within* to that which is 'outside' of us. It occurs in a way that transcends subject and object. We call it beauty.

Beauty also heals.

That's partly why and how:

Men become beautiful dancers of joy.

Men always marvel at the *divine* motion of a woman dancing because her motion carries joy as beauty in ways that reveal the living promise of love defined as promise kept.

Males enviously watch *how* men dance.

Males imitate men but without the authenticity of creative involvement because males haven't learned how to unite self-depth and expressiveness with open hands, heart, body, and mind: they haven't learned *the moves* in living that reveal the beauties of life.

So, back to basics:

Male incompleteness means not doing what a male is meant to do—become a man.

Male incompleteness hollows the heart, mind, and spirit.

Male incompleteness is observable as *male discontent*.

A male in discontent should not seek a mate until the right questions have been asked and answered honestly, followed by unalterably sincere actions to change all negative habits, attitudes, and behaviors in preparation for re-asking the same questions over and over and over for growth.

A male in discontent is insecure. That's not the problem. The problem is he's reluctant to discuss his discontent and do something about it because of fear and no answers to....

THE BASIC QUESTIONS

they are:

+ Am I a young male becoming an aging male?

+ Am I a pretend male?

+ Am I an aging male?

+ If I'm an aging male, why am I not a man?

+ If I pose as a man, why do I do that?

+ If I'm a young male, am I really interested in becoming a man?

+ If I'm an older male, am I truly and deeply willing to change *anything* about myself?

+ Am I willing to be deeply self-honest?

+ What are the criteria for maturity?

+ Am I immature?

✦ Can I accurately and fully discuss maturity and my immaturity?

✦ How do I hide my immaturity?

✦ Am I truly and deeply motivated to achieve maturity?

✦ Am I deeply motivated *at all*?

✦ Was my father a man, my mother a woman? Or were they male and female in habit and in wedlock, divorced, or gone?

✦ Do I deeply respect my parents? Do I overestimate them? Do I even like them?

✦ How well do I really know my parents?

✦ How am I negatively like either or both of my parents?

✦ Who are my truest parents?

✦ What are the principles I live by and do not compromise?

✦ Can I define 'principle' and name five?

✦ What do I value most, not intellectually, generally, or abstractly, but really?

✦ Can I define value?

+ How do I honor my values with action?

+ How negatively selfish and negatively stubborn am I?

+ Do I lie? Am I a liar? Am I shallow in any way?

+ Can I be deeply *trusted*? Is my word my bond?

+ Do I really understand what the word selfish signifies positively and negatively related to my behavior, attitude, language, time, money, body, and spirit?

+ What sacrifices am I deeply able/willing and ready to make for a truly good way of living?

+ What am I willing to lose?

+ How do I define 'good living' apart from money and comfort?

+ Do I procrastinate? If so, why?

+ Am I cowardly about *anything*?

+ To what extent does fear influence me?

+ Am I afraid of commitment, involvement, and deep intimacy?

+ Am I afraid of really deep, all the way love?

+ If I am afraid, am I willing to confront my fears completely and take on the pain of growing?

✦ Do I honor all information related to my mental, physical, and spiritual health and do I *apply it all fully*?

✦ Am I arrogant?

✦ Do I study *anything* to understand the valid truths of spiritual inquiry?

✦ On what important issues and topics do I reflect openly, without habitual bias?

✦ Am I interested in really learning how to think realistically?

✦ Am I unnecessarily critical and judgmental?

✦ When I'm sixty what will I have accomplished and achieved?

✦ When I'm seventy what will I value most, and will I have become a man in the continuity of becoming a man? Or will I be a modified version of my father or other males?

✦ When I'm eighty what will I revere most?

✦ When I'm ninety what will I say?

✦ If I don't make it to age fifty, what am I doing *now* to make living good for me and for those I say I love?

+ If I become a parent, am I the complete example of what I want my children to become in their own ways?

+ Am I wisely honest?

+ Am I a self-example of all I admire?

+ Do I know one *man*?

+ What is *my* definition of a man?

+ When I say I'm sorry, do I *really mean it* enough not to repeat what I did?

+ Am I a manipulator of persons without admitting it?

+ Am I truly reliable?

+ Do I really keep my word to myself and to others?

+ Am I primarily kind, gentle, and tender?

+ Do I *fully apply* what I already know that would make living better?

+ Do I listen openly and willingly without interrupting?

+ Do I give openly, willingly, fully, and *wisely*? If not, why?

✦ Am I able to forgive?

✦ Do my fears and feelings govern me more than I admit?

✦ Do I make decisions primarily because of feelings?

✦ Do I know how to think accurately and make truly good decisions?

✦ Why do I think the way I think?

✦ What's distorted in the way I think?

✦ What are my conflicts?

✦ How am I sick?

✦ Do I want to heal?

✦ Am I actively determined to resolve my personal conflicts so I don't mess up again and again and hurt the ones I say I love?

✦ Do I have persons in my life I truly love? Or am I just loyal?

✦ Do I even know what true and lasting love is and what it takes to make it happen for the long haul?

✦ What do I really want, then really, really want?

✦ Are my wants shallow and unrealistic?

✦ Am I fooling myself about any personal dreams?

+ Do I have any dreams?

+ Are my personal dreams truly mine to dream— the ones I'm supposed to be dreaming?

+ What do I need?

+ Am I *needy*?

+ Do I hide my neediness?

+ Do I burden others with problems only I can solve?

+ Do I overestimate my maturity, kindness, and sincerity?

+ Do I impose my way of thinking on others then rationalize my position to retain my way of doing things?

+ What's most important to me—where do I put my energy and attention *first*, every day?

+ What is my primary *mission*?

+ What are the special events I will make occur in living so I can genuinely and meaningfully look back and say 'I did it' and 'I loved'?

so....to reiterate:

If the basic questions are not fully answered as actions, then a male will remain mostly male—adapted to his incompleteness and degrees of discontent.

A man expects pain and learns how to integrate it positively without self-waste or the waste of others.

A man knows pain and inconvenience are his allies.

A man is supremely vulnerable but equally strong. Therefore:

How he lives *matters*.

How he seeks *matters*.

What he seeks *matters*.

What he studies *matters* because the questions he asks *matter* and his answers *matter*.

A man knows human reality is dominated by grisliness due to ignorance and immaturity.

He knows destiny depends on the dignity and integrity of self in actions for maximum experiences of greater meanings shared.

He knows destiny is not fate.

He knows fate is the predictable aspects of negligence.

He knows tragedy is blindness due to ignorance and/or negligence.

consider....

Males often think argumentativeness is an aspect of being reasonable. It's not. It's weakness due to discontent, imitation, ignorance, fear, and habit.

Unreasonable is a way of functioning that uses smooth or more blatant arguing to preserve control by securing an adversary's submission, even if the adversary is self.

Reasonable presumes better mental health and the use of open reasoning.

i know....

Pure power has *made* each of us a womb for the birth of what we create that's truly good.

All abuse is the use of power weakened into force by a weak person.

A man knows that love is like an infant.

A man will never knowingly or willingly hurt an infant or a child in any way. He knows that violation is a deep word, mutilation is deeper, and infanticide is the rape and destruction of Creation.

A man will kneel to outer space, to the seemingly most trivial aspects of the natural world, to his own species, and to the simplest of gestures, particularly the gentle outreach of a very young hand. Then a man will kneel to his beloved.

A man and woman know that the basic experience of the spiritual is simple. It includes the physical as good health and beautiful pleasures, the mental as good health and open reasoning, and spirit as that which causes the *will* to do on earth, with *desire* and for love, as it is in what we casually call *heaven*.

This means men and women enjoy living *boldly* and *honestly*; then they take it all to the children, and *give* it to them.

blunt male/female facts:

No male can claim a female as 'my *woman*' and no female can claim a male as 'my *man*'. Each can only say 'this is my female' or 'this is my male'....or chick or guy or significant other or mate or spouse or husband or wife or boyfriend or girlfriend, lover, one-nighter, or meat.

Only a male will call a female a bitch or 'my bitch' or 'my girl'.

Only a male will call a female a cunt, a whore, slut, or pussy.

Only a male will use the word motherfucker.

Only a male will say fuck you to a female.

Only a male will condescend to a female.

Only a male will use a female for sex.

Only a female will tolerate and imitate male behavior.

Only a male or a female will neglect a child.

Only a male or female will play games with love.

Only a male or female will argue rather than discuss.

Please know:

Man and woman are words that denote ***achievement***. That stature must be earned and sustained. Without the distinction of that achievement, both words lose dignity and, therefore, depth of meaning....the way it is in today's world. Everywhere.

Listen to others and to yourself for how often you hear, say, read, or think the words man, woman, men, women.

If you become an old man instead of an old male, you'll know—

You were not fragile, only vulnerable.

You did not impose on others.

You challenged any force that could reduce the potential for love.

You learned that the most challenging tasks of living are to triumph over gauntlet, conquer self positively, and greet reality and relationships fully.

You tried very hard to maintain clear perspectives and keep the now pure.

Yes, if you become an old man instead of an old male, you'll know—

You learned that your 'vision' became contextual—dominated by the 'bigger picture'—so you could connect the dots of numerous perspectives and apply that clarity to the little picture called daily living.

You did your best to *make* love for those you loved and *met*.

You learned to study, listen, and think to enhance perception before engagement became endeavor.

You learned to be patient in conversations and not interrupt.

You learned how a child invites a parent to class so the parent can learn more about the sanctity of vitality.

You learned how to mature and how to love with childlike simplicity centered in the miracles of the obvious.

You learned why we seek engagement with actual and symbolic 'children' and our things—because children and things can revitalize and restore the living presence of the question of God in us: physically, emotionally, rationally, concretely, and spiritually.

You let children teach you.

You named each day good.

You learned how to take care of other living beings.

You learned you are what you do with what you discover.

You learned how discoveries determine how you hide and what you seek.

You learned how to seek without hiding.

You learned that yes is gathered fully only if you deal with all the problems....

THAT PERTAIN TO MALE DISCONTENT

IF YOU'RE CURIOUS about the long haul....

If you argue easily....

If you're awake between 2 and 5 a.m. and you feel more alone/frustrated/confused than you like.... and you take a drink, a pill, smoke weed, get on the Internet, watch tv, listen to music, check your cell phone, and feel angry more than you like....

If you brood, stay away from deeper intimacy, avoid commitment, home, and children more than you like....

If you have intercourse without love or with your hand more than you like....

If you wish maybe you'd done things differently or had better answers....

If you don't know what to do to feel happier, more positive, more capable....

If you go through any of this often, in or out of wedlock, older or younger, you're in discontent.

If you defend yourself against criticism, you're in discontent.

If you're stubborn and don't admit your mistakes and really change your ways, starting with your health habits, how you talk or shut down or blame or criticize, you're in discontent.

Ever wish you hadn't screamed at your girlfriend or wife or mate or partner or ex, friend, dog, or been a jerk to someone, to your child or children, or to a stranger?

Ever experience road rage or real intense impatience *a lot*?

Ever feel like crap for working too hard or not hard enough and/or neglecting the people *you-say-you-love*?

Ever been passive about love when you should have been active but you just-didn't-do-it?

Ever acknowledge you're a manipulator who is smooth and practiced, a good liar to others, and a better liar to yourself?

Are you sarcastic when you should be compassionate and centered?

If you want to change but you don't, why not?

it's all a matter of:

Courage, coward, male, man, mature, immature, sick or healing: it's that cut and dry. What do you want?

Choose what you want. If you don't, time will choose for you. That means you'll lose.

please know these facts:

The consequences of courage or coward are as predictable as the turning of the earth.

Spotting cowardice is as easy as seeing raindrops on dry cement.

Males married to making money find ways to avoid full-on self-acknowledgement and exposure of that marriage.

Male marriage to making money is not subject to divorce.

Money-males usually deny marriage to making money.

Money-males will not commit any infidelity, deceit, or betrayal of their $ beloved.

Money-males often try to include wedlock and offspring. They fail. Money wins.

Whatever you treasure, that's primarily where your heart is.

You'll do what's important to you no matter how you explain/justify/defend why you do what you do. All that matters to you is protecting what you treasure.

A whole lotta males treasure more treasure and never ask if it's valid treasure.

All actions reveal priorities and position—where you stand, for what, and with whom. Your actions define you every day.

Discontented males rule the world.

All males do not understand a man's power, but they recognize it. And it makes them pause. It can make the world pause.

so, for the male in discontent....

The only way to restore true and deep vitality is to say it like it is then get some humble going on so you can surrender to the facts and change how you function.

No faking it. Learn appreciative humility: the *active* love that makes you and others truly important. If you fake it, fake wins and you become just another individual losing what shouldn't be lost.

Do it for real: stay sensitive and hooked in to the little things that reveal how you really care; no going through the motions and saying a lot of words and putting some feeling to it all so it seems real enough to bypass criticism.

Do it for real or move on with your discontent. That means you won't really go anywhere except in your car.

Learning about humility will cause frustration and challenges that aren't easy to cope with or tolerate. But if you're willing to deal with that, humility will bring a self-sunrise. And the pain of that dawn will break you and release you into your potential for goodness: things will get a little brighter as time passes and you'll smile more sincerely. That's what true 'light' always does if you give it full permission to do its thing: it penetrates you, breaks you, and readies you for deeper freedom. Otherwise, your brightness is a flashlight and you're just another battery with limited juice.

True light will *place* you on a cold, moon-bright desert where you *know* you're alone, anonymous, utterly insignificant and significant, and completely helpless and powerful within the confusing implications of the lights and darks all around you and in you. You will understand that you are *in **your freedom***. That's how big and miraculous your position will be: a confrontation with your own power, and you *know* it. That's how *awe* occurs. And why you will cry.

Thus positioned, you will learn that your choices make all the difference because choice is the only true transportation available to more light casually called tomorrow.

but....

You must *choose* because light doesn't hang around waiting for you to catch up. If it's not received and chosen, it leaves without you.

Without true light, you will seek false light, the lie.
You must choose light or the lie.

if you choose light you will learn....

Sunrise of self is *the **state of grace***.

Grace makes great but simple demands that begin with self in *vow* to deep self-honesty: authenticity versus ambiguity, realistic versus unrealistic.

To avoid the demands of this grace is to fall.

To fall is to die.

The world is profoundly crowded with the noises of the falling and the behaviors of the dying.

Without this grace, aging males shrivel and young males flounder, flail, and become beauty tethered to a pole in high wind. Eventually, beauty fades, shreds, and goes. All that's left is another aging male drifting away to old.

so, if you're interested in ending your discontent, you'll have to....

Decide whether you're willing to stand in your night alone until you see light in the dark of you. This personal situation is the major genesis-risk and the deepest reality of motivation-risk for the deepest personal yes to living better. Yes means 'I'll take the risks, full-on, 100 percent'.

You'll need strong hands to hold your heart, spirit, and words in place so you can stay positioned to feel and see the light begin to open you. If you let it happen, you will have begun the courage to become a man sustaining the beauty of who you are through what you *genuinely* do for love in every action. This is the essence of greatest faith in all of its implications for every human on the planet.

In today's world, that kind of great faith is radical because it's so simple and so rare.

That said....

It's never too late to begin unless you're not available. Then it *is* too late because you don't want to learn:

How to plant a seed in the universe and watch it grow some love;

That the universe is womb for child;

That no other word in any language signifies God more than 'child', and that no other word in any language signifies womb's reality more than 'woman'.

So....

If you don't want to learn any of that, you won't enjoy knowing, through a woman, that the history of the universe is in her womb and, therefore, in her heart. She carries it all. That's why a woman is so wonderful and powerful. And why she must be revered, always.

A man learns this with increasing clarity and depth. And he learns about the holiness of womb everywhere, even when meeting another person, or looking in the mirror.

A man learns that his greatest achievement is to teach and train a child to understand and respond to the demands of reality appropriately, strongly, humbly, and consistently in preparation for the best uses of freedom. He places his freedom in service to womb. He is the example of what he teaches.

A woman knows that her greatest achievement is to teach and train a child to understand and respond to structure, action, and interaction appropriately, clearly, and consistently in preparation for further training.

A woman naturally places her freedom in service to womb, whether she is able to bear children or not.

All men and women marry, even if they remain celibate.

Celibate men and women marry life's greatest meanings and express them through actions that *make* love from love's potential in self, for others, and with the environment. From this love comes 'the children' of their creativity.

The personal absence of any 'children' always produces deep discontent and the motion of a slow emptiness leading to submission and the opening of quiet despair—like sitting on a narrow ledge at a thousand feet, legs dangling. It takes eight to ten seconds for a tossed stone to hit bottom. The falling stone is a meaningless action until you relate to it. Either you follow the stone or you return to *life* through better living. Those are the alternatives. No options. You look around at all the world and you know you must choose. To sit is not an option. Sitting means you followed the stone without moving.

In contrast to man and woman....

Males and females who become aging males and females remain busy in a mildly delusional opaqueness of being where stubborn desperation and unnatural aloneness convert the magnificence of beauty into waned, faded, atrophied, and almost forgotten experiences confined to trace memories that evoke painful nostalgia within the burdensome fullness of knowing: 'I had it all ahead of me back then....what happened?'

Aging males and females do not fully learn that:

Success is adventure driven by desire for the possible and the positive.

Success is nearly anonymous because its essence is invisible.

Success is affirmation beyond fear and doubt.

Success is made in those you truly love.

Success is fulfillment as service.

Success is in maturing.

Success is rare.

If we don't die young, we all know these fact-fragments:

We will work, make purchases, and pay bills.

We will marry legally, stay married, divorce, remarry, or remain single.

We will be heterosexual, bisexual, homosexual, transsexual, or transgender.

We will be negligent and stubborn.

We will include and exclude, be included and excluded.

We will make decisions and draw conclusions based on assumptions.

We will be ill in varying degrees of seriousness.

We will encounter our emotional issues.

We will or will not deal with our emotional issues honestly, actively, and fully.

We will experience the effects of our mental health.

We will procrastinate.

We will cheat.

We will increasingly encounter the reality of mortality.

We will experience disease and/or surgery.

We will betray trust.

We will lie.

We will suffer.

We will spend money.

We will have dental work.

We will have gas, diarrhea, constipation, and nausea.

We will be informed of others' deaths.

We will worry.

We will experience anxiety.

We will experience sex.

We will learn to think, plan, and love in varying degrees of completion.

We will say 'I will die'.

We will say I love you.

Additional fact-fragments that add up:

The greatest persons are made great by the quality and scope of their yes.

The greatest persons are *deeply vital* persons. They initial the wind without using the alphabet. They stand *alone,* and with those they love. They defend truth only. They do not fight. They declare war. The battle cry is in the eyes: 100 percent yes. Then they do it. This greatness is most often observable in a woman. It is masterfully simple and dominated beautifully by the priority of love not governed by emotion or diminished by reasoning.

Greatness of person requires:

Love and humor;
Teaching and learning;
Compassion and honesty;
Mastery and humility;
Strength and courage.

In contrast:

Humankind is a fugitive from courage.
Humankind is dominated by aging males.
Humankind is in discontent.
Womankind is more stable, centered, and loving.
Childkind is sunrise.
Babykind is sun.

Side note: in America....

Pleasure and love are often confused and separated—
Frosting is pleasure.
Love is cake.
Frosting wins.
Males want the frosting.
Men want the cake *with* frosting. So a man makes cake with a woman. They frost it together.

Males don't care where or how the cake is baked as long as they get a piece.

Consider....

Who do you follow, who do you lead, and why?

If you follow, can you *lead*?

If you don't follow anyone or anything, or lead someone, what's going on?

Would I want you with me on a survival team?

Would you want you on a survival team?

Would I want you to care for my child's mind, spirit, and body with complete trust that all three would be nurtured and protected because of your unquestionable maturity, alertness, sensitivity, and ability to make only the best decisions? If you answer no to any of the questions, what in you is missing?

To reiterate *facts forward*:

When we're humbly in the presence of an infant or child, we are in prayer and in divinity. Any person unable to experience that prayer fully is not fully receptive to the divinity of children, even if you are a parent. If that person is you, you're messed up.

Womb is omnipresent.

To become a man, a male must be taught to respect all wombs—all persons, creatures, natures, true facts, true truths, and self.

Respect and responsibility demand service to love.

We know what love is by its absence.

Adaptation to the absence and/or reduction of love further distorts love. Increased distortions of love cause perversions of love.

Perversions of love are destructive.

Perversions of love are normalized and integrated personally and culturally.

Perversions of love occur in houses of worship, homes, businesses, politics, on the street, in homes, in beds, in language, in entertainment, and in legal systems—in all cultures and societies, in all institutions, and in all ways where arbitrary or biased reasoning is preferred over the quest for realistic love and justice.

Neglect of love in any way is the beginning of greed and arrogance.

All species are perfectly suited for the conditions of their environment.

Humankind is not suited perfectly for anything environmentally. For what then is humankind perfectly suited? The only answer: learning how to think and how to love.

Humankind has no tangible home. Love is our only home, the only 'place' where we can truly and most deeply live. It is the ultimate shelter and destiny.

All humans must 'make' love or die alive in a fall without motion toward disappearance without absence.

Self-waste is the way of the world, and the way of the world is increasingly centered on information, construction, development, and advancements rather than on valid growth toward the deeply meaningful new: progress.

The immaturity of older males is defined by and confined to negatively stubborn thinking and defensiveness. This fact includes all levels of aging male, from street to world leader. Immaturity is disastrously ubiquitous.

America is beginning to suffer fully from a proliferation of aging males and younger males pretending to be men.

American culture increasingly reflects the concerns, attitudes, desires, actions, and behaviors of boys becoming aging males in positions requiring the skills, training, courage, strength, maturity, and mastery of men.

Males master skills but do not fully apply the dynamic of mastery to the demands of learning how to think, love, and live. This aspect of protracted *boyishness* is the unintended presence of chronic immaturity becoming arrogant cowardice in an aging body.

All males, when hearing a man speak, will listen and know their place. Males intimidated by a man will challenge boldly or subtly, dismiss, compliment, criticize, and/or tolerate him one way or another. A male interested in becoming a man will somehow try to meet a man, ask questions, and listen openly.

Men and women struggle to learn beyond the narrow confines of misrepresented religion and its equally narrow practitioners mired in outdated and unrealistic interpretations of matters spiritual.

Men and women rightly reject males and females who pimp the question of Spirit, reduce its stature, pollute its dignity, cynically eviscerate its beauties, and reshape its realities.

The global effect of the collective male in discontent is predictable and tragic. It promises increased manless-ness and more destructiveness because:

The male does not accept womb as his responsibility because....

The male cannot see well. So....

He has little active interest in vision or re-vision, which means....

He is broadly puerile—

He prefers safety and control because at some level of awareness he perceives that he is functionally extraneous and of less significance than any....

Woman

The word means....

Superior to man.

This fact is based on her honesty, strength, capacity for love, and capability to love: woman is very realistic.

Men know this.

Young male knows this.

All pretend males and aging males know this but in their own ways deny it through assertions of the opposite: the superiority of the male.

A woman is a great and sacred womb. Men know this.

A woman transcends the criteria for manhood. Men know this.

This is due to *one quality*. Every female on the planet carries this quality. When this quality activates a female, not only does she become herself, she also recognizes what becoming a woman means. She learns she is the mother in Creation's womb. And she learns that when she loves, she gives to her chosen receiver the birth of love. Her touch is magical. She heals. Her presence contains the promises of divinity. Her actions keep those promises. She can do this because of one quality she alone *naturally* carries—the wild beauty of the holy.

All males, including the cynical, the bitter and hard, the arrogant, the young, the aging, the old, and the destructive cannot escape the reality of the holiness she carries. They can only deny it, reject it, or crush it.

This holiness is what *men* want to protect in their daughters, and what they want to teach their sons to protect and respect in *any* female, anywhere, anytime. So they teach their sons to see a female as a potential woman, one who carries love naturally. They teach their sons to *honor* the female.

Women teach their daughters to look in a full-length mirror for wholeness, for more than a face and a maturing body.

They teach their daughters to see their potential as a gift to be brought forth—the gift on which the whole world relies.

They teach their daughters to carry the truth, beauty, and proof of what every great religion strives to express—the whole reality of what the word God most broadly, specifically, and beautifully denotes.

That reality is held in the innocence and sanctity of the female.

Held and waiting.

Women teach this to their daughters.

To all males:

Whenever you see a *female*—young, older, or old, anywhere and in any condition—honor her by remembering what she carries; and never abuse it by abusing her *in-any-way*.

Every womb is holy, even if it does not produce a biological child. The holiness of its keeper, the female, naturally makes it so.

Whether you are attracted, angered, repulsed, or neutral, honor every female as a bearer and keeper of holiness for the birth of love. Demonstrate how you honor her by offering to her your genuine respect and courtesy.

And:

Whenever you meet a *woman,* find a way to kneel while you stare.

With that in mind....

When you believe you've fallen in love, let the fullness of your desire be based solely on that wonderfully observable holiness she carries in readiness to share *with you*. Maybe. This is her greatest beauty, her greatest truth. Honor what she carries by never using or abusing her spirit or her body and all that she can offer.... because no matter what you have to offer, it's always inferior to her gift and her love for you. If that's not true for you, then your fall into love is shallow. It is intense romance in preparation for the fall of parting and, eventually, wishing you hadn't.

Falling in love most deeply means, above all else, loving the love the other person *is*. It means developing the courage to grow into that love fully.

Falling deeply in love and fully into love is a free-fall with no possibility of injury, ever. It brings absolute trust.

Man facts:

Men know how to honor holiness and holiness in a woman.

When men witness pregnancy fulfilled as birth, birth tells the man his status within creation: functional; his seed and assistance are required. And he surrenders.

A man completes the portrait of himself through his demeanor as 'father' because it fills him with ultimate purpose: to become the 'womb' of man-love through which the future of *family* will be born and sustained. That future entails the wellness and wellbeing of family, and the evolving structures for teaching the child/children how to think and love so each child can secure in their futures what they have witnessed in the *home*. This priority responsibility guides him more deeply into the wild beauty of love, step by step.

So....

He surrenders: he has no urge to compete with a woman.

He knows he cannot compete with a woman.

He knows that to compete with her is self-waste in the extreme.

He knows he would lose. Lose everything.

A man knows woman *is* the home and that he is its keeper for *her*.

All of this means:

A woman *carries* God. A man discovers God.

A man discovers woman. A woman includes a man.

All men know this. All males know this.

And:

A woman will love a man more than her children but less than her children. And men know they are *her* children deeply shared with him; he knows it is she who brings Creation into time for all to see—birth as purity in action and motherhood in complete devotion.

The full integrity of being is on display through her; it is the natural labor of love's effort to reproduce itself in the form of being we casually call human. And she does it all naturally.

A man knows a woman can *live* without him. He can't say that about her because every man longs for the treasure called woman. So, he waits, looks, and hopes that, one day, he will be in the presence of she who will say to him this part of her—

Monologue On Love....

'I am strong. I am durable. I am vulnerable but I am not fragile. I do not fall apart under stress or give in to pain. I endure. I have learned how to be a woman. I am a woman. Know that.

You can trust me completely. I will never betray you in any way. I will work for you and with you, never against you. I will provide full love for you because I am able to do that, willing to do that, filled with the love necessary to do that, and I deeply desire to do that.

I will never be harsh to you.

I will never belittle you.

I will never speak sarcastically to you.

I will always be honest with you. No aspect of who I am or what I feel will be private. You will know it all, all the time. That means you will know me.

I will do this because....

I love you. My love for you is deep. I offer my time, body, hands, and commitment to *you*. You are my vow.

I want *your* touch, voice, and eyes. I want you. I open my world to you, always. You have my pleasure before I give it because your pleasure is *my* pleasure. And if a time comes when you can no longer pleasure me, I will still love you, love you as I do now, and I will give my pleasure to you *joyfully*.

I love to feel your lips caress my cheeks and forehead, breasts, and flower.

I love to feel you.

I love to give whatever I can to make you happy.

I make myself ripe and fragrant daily, to be harvested and enjoyed by *you*. Yes, I prepare my flesh for you. I lift my breasts and hold them....my belly I reveal....all for you. All I am, I give to you. I present myself for your love the way I present my spirit as living prayer daily in the holy now that tells me how to receive, and receive what you give while I offer me for our journey through hands, fingers, arms, legs, kiss, caress, and all manner of openness until we join and hold, hold into that precious moment when time takes us into itself as raw beauty and pure delight in the wild. I am exclusively yours in the wild until the day I die. I will never be tamed.

My love for you is in all I do, and what I do I do for you.

I ask you to take me into your love and *make* me.... *again and again*....for I am yours, yours alone. My sweet, love is what love does or love is what love was. And that 'was' from me will never be....for my love *is*.

Love me hard, sweet, wild, and slow. And when you love me over and over, whisper what I should know.

Imperfect I am, yes, but perfect is my vow to *love* you, love you always, as I do now.

Can you see me? If so, tell me how. *Tell* me. Like I tell the flowers I see, you tell me.

If I can love you better than I do now, tell me, oh tell me please tell me how.

What are your words, my sweet?

If you love me as I love you, you will give me your heart while I give mine. I will carry your heart and you will carry mine. And we will protect each other that way.

I'm trembling....so listen closely: in early morning when God talks sacred story, I waken and *feel* the language. I see wide sky blue announce the precious where and why of beauty as beauty offered now.

That is how I offer you my seasons, desire, and delight. I offer it all now. I lay down my life, lift up my dreams, and give all my days and all my breath to you. Now. So, hold me and speak. Tell me....tell me what you most truly feel. Please. Whisper what in you for me is *most* real, most *true*. And watch my eyes. Talk to me deep, deep from your heart. And do it *now*. If you cannot do that....leave.'

MAN

Criteria: a man is—

- ✦ Masculine
- ✦ Rugged
- ✦ Honest & Direct
- ✦ Unpretentious
- ✦ Protective of Women, Children, The Old
- ✦ Courageous
- ✦ Strong
- ✦ Trustworthy
- ✦ Adaptable
- ✦ Lover To A Beloved
- ✦ A True Friend

Definitions of The Criteria:

Masculine: realistic, patient, responsible, calmly attentive, empathic, and compassionate; action ready, survival driven; a lover of living and his beloved; a lover of intimacy; a protector of life; a seeker and doer; able to forgive.

Rugged: firm, independently decisive, gracious and durable under pressure, willing and able to sacrifice for the truly good.

Honest & Direct: fearless of commitment; reliable; no lies, no deception, evasiveness, or betrayal of trust.

Unpretentious: has no pose or costume.

Protective: defers to women, children, and the old with time, energy, and money; family first; no physical, verbal, or spiritual abuse, ever.

Courageous: able to see, affirm, and fight for the truly good.

Strong: takes action without procrastination; able to lead, able to follow.

Trustworthy: his word is his bond.

Adaptable: thinks before speaking and acting; serves only the best decisions.

Lover: a partner and companion for family and the pleasures that define love; pursues the ultimately important; provides for family beyond dying.

True Friend: shares deeply and trustingly.

That is all a man can do, and it takes all a man can do to do it all. He can never do it all perfectly. So he strives, knowing that his efforts will fill him with the content of the following:

Ethics as respect and actions for the dignity of life and living: persons, animals, nature, and the divine.

Faith as learning how to preserve and increase the proliferation of genuine love.

Pleasure as participation in true goodness related to love.

Reflection as it nurtures the development of intuition to be used as the 'light' for aging amid the paradoxes and pains of living toward dying.

Perfection as it signifies the quest for *mastery* and the maintenance of love's integrity.

A man lives to say this part of his....

Monologue On Love....

'Of love and desire let no man speak
Until that union has made him weak'.

For me to say that to you required that I conquer me. I have done that. I have learned. I have trained. I am ready for love. I am ready for *you*. Only you. You ask me to speak, to tell you my heart and mind. I am telling you now, telling you of love, my love; telling you of desire, my desire. Their union has made me weak. I claim that weakness by surrendering to you. Only you. Love, time, desire, and you are united in me. That is my weakness. It is my strength.

I desire you.
I desire you in all ways.
I want *you* in all ways.
I have chosen you.
I will receive you completely. And I will remain.

I am before you now, waiting.
I am ready to exchange lives.
I am ready to engage with you. Only you. My heart is a vow. I give it to you.

I will do this for you: wrap you in my strength, courage, and love; secure you against the cold, wind, heat, and fire of human ways and words; hold you as my sunrise and kneel with you at sunset when light talks of Truth against darkness and the loss of love, and against the reckless drive of wasted motion—when love seems divided into shards of Above and below, leaving only Apple and Compass, Cross and Star to combat the lords, hordes, and hounds of war. I will kneel with you and I will stand with you against all of that.

Therefore, this is my heart, my vow:

I will for you: be present.
I will for you: listen, always.
I will for you: conquer me, always.
I will for you: seek and provide.
I will for you: lie awake at night and stare at you.
I will for you: provide the depth of human trust.
I will for you: seek your nectar.
I will for you: drink deeply.
I will for you: touch, caress, and linger.
I will for you: dance.
I will for you: laugh.
I will for you: sing.
I will for you: be me.
I will for you: rely on you.
I will for you: receive you wholly.

I will for you: thrill you. I will make your body sing. And there I will remain until you laugh, cry, and make the sound of holding me with your song.

If these words strike you as unrealistic or sentimental, then your heart cannot embrace my heart, ways, and weapons.

If these words seem to be no more than poetic aspiration, no more than the loosened idealisms of an immature romantic, then you do not see my heart, ways, and weapons.

If these words do not provide for you the reality of who I am for you, then you do not have the heart you say you prize. And your words to me are false, unworthy of this offer. Unworthy of me. Choose.

Conclusion

This is the end of the book. I'm sitting in this cabin. October began with the coldest cold snap in ninety years. My heating isn't hooked up yet so it was a *cold* week.

I've been thinking how best to finish up.
No more to say.
This is it. The book's done.

What do I *really know*?
Well, I know....

Man is the world's mule and sun to heaven's earth and grace—woman.

United, they produce child, the mystery of divinity for all to see.

And to each other they say with word and action:

> 'Receive from me the promise of sky,
> And rest me with you that I may die
> Having given to you all my hours
> Now holding rain for all your flowers'.

71656990R00134

Made in the USA
San Bernardino, CA
17 March 2018